Selected Poems

Wallace Stevens

Selected Poems

Edited by John N. Serio

ALFRED A. KNOPF   *New York*   2009

Poems included in this collection were originally published in the following works:
Harmonium, copyright © 1923 by Alfred A. Knopf, Inc., and renewed 1951
by Wallace Stevens. Copyright © 1931 by Wallace Stevens and renewed 1959
by Elsie Stevens and Holly Stephenson (Alfred A. Knopf).
Ideas of Order, copyright © 1936 by Wallace Stevens and renewed 1964
by Holly Stevens (Alfred A. Knopf).
The Man with the Blue Guitar, copyright © 1935, 1936, 1937 by Wallace Stevens and
renewed 1964, 1965 by Holly Stevens (Alfred A. Knopf).
Parts of a World, copyright © 1942 by Wallace Stevens and renewed 1970
by Holly Stevens (Alfred A. Knopf).
Transport to Summer, copyright © 1947 by Wallace Stevens and renewed 1974
by Holly Stevens (Alfred A. Knopf).
The Auroras of Autumn, copyright © 1950 by Wallace Stevens and
renewed 1977 by Holly Stevens (Alfred A. Knopf).
The Collected Poems of Wallace Stevens, copyright © 1954 by Wallace Stevens and
renewed 1982 by Holly Stevens (Alfred A. Knopf).
Opus Posthumous, copyright © 1957 by Elsie Stevens and Holly Stevens and
renewed 1985 by Holly Stevens (Alfred A. Knopf).
The Necessary Angel, copyright © 1951 by Wallace Stevens and renewed 1979
by Holly Stevens (Alfred A. Knopf).

Library of Congress Cataloging-in-Publication Data
Stevens, Wallace, 1879–1955.
[Poems. Selections]
Selected poems / by Wallace Stevens ; edited by John Serio. — 1st ed.
p. cm.
Includes bibliographical references and index.
ISBN 978-0-307-28047-3
I. Serio, John N., 1943– II. Title.
PS3537.T4753A6 2009
811'.52—dc22   2009000505

Manufactured in the United States of America
First Edition

Contents

FROM *Transport to Summer* (1947)

Introduction

1

What can one say about a poet who writes, quite tenderly, "And for what, except for you, do I feel love?" and who does not mean his wife, or his daughter, or any other person, but rather an imaginary figure: the muse? But that is how Wallace Stevens begins the prologue to what many consider his greatest poem, "Notes Toward a Supreme Fiction"—with a passionate, intimate address not to a beloved but to an intangible concept: inspiration. With something approaching erotic fervor, Stevens personifies an abstraction and speaks directly to poetry, as if it were his lover:

> In the uncertain light of single, certain truth,
> Equal in living changingness to the light
> In which I meet you, in which we sit at rest,
> For a moment in the central of our being,
> The vivid transparence that you bring is peace.

No other poet I know of has written so elegantly and so persuasively about the beauty and significance of poetry in everyday life. We find these declarations not only in Stevens's poems but also in his essays, most of which originated as invited lectures on the subject of poetry. In these essays, Stevens seduces us with his enchanting prose to believe in the spiritual importance of poetry. The imagination—frequently synonymous with the act of the mind, or poetry, for Stevens—is what gives life its savor, its sanction, its sacred quality. In a passage from "The Noble Rider and the Sound of Words," he stresses the importance of poetic language by evoking our human craving for the sound of words:

> The deepening need for words to express our thoughts and feelings which, we are sure, are all the truth that we shall ever experience, having no illusions, makes us listen to words when we hear them, loving them and feeling them, makes us search the

sound of them, for a finality, a perfection, an unalterable vibration, which it is only within the power of the acutest poet to give them.[1]

Noting that the imagination (poetry) must be based on reality, and furthermore that the interdependence of the imagination and reality is crucial, Stevens goes on to isolate poetry's inherent distinctiveness: It bestows nobility, a quality he defines as "our spiritual height and depth" (664). Nobility emerges from the press of the imagination against a world that seems chaotic, crass, violent, and banal. The task of the poet is to transmit his imaginative power to others. Stevens sees the poet fulfilling himself "only as he sees his imagination become the light in the minds of others." Simply put, the poet's role "is to help people to live their lives" (660–1).

One could cite other essays that make Stevens's case for poetry, but the real question is: How well does his own poetry measure up to his ideal? After all, the telling phrase in the opening line of the invocation to "Notes Toward a Supreme Fiction" is "except for you." Since the "you" refers to the creative faculty of the mind, it excludes everything else, including, of course, people. At the very least, such devotion to art rather than another person might strike a reader as odd. It has certainly struck many readers as cold and impersonal. With such observations as the following, Stevens has done little to alter that impression: "Life is not people and scene but thought and feeling" (909); "Life is an affair of people not of places. But for me life is an affair of places and that is the trouble" (901); "I have no life except in poetry" (913).

There is an abstract feature to much of Stevens's poetry that distinguishes it from that of most other poets. Modern lyric poets, for example, usually write about more tangible topics, often using the first-person singular. One thinks of the speaker contrasting his neighbor's view of walls with his own in Robert Frost's "Mending Wall," or the persona's sudden reversal of perspective toward a rather ugly, lice-infested fish in Elizabeth Bishop's "The Fish," or even the paralyzing insecurity of T. S. Eliot's J. Alfred Prufrock, dreading a social encounter ("In the room the women come and go / Talking of Michelangelo").[2] Each of these poems has a well-defined speaker and a clear setting. Each invites the reader to identify with or relate to the principal human figure in the poem.

By contrast, Stevens's poems frequently seem bizarre, theoretical, and detached. What is one to make of lines such as "The only emperor is the emperor of ice-cream"; or "A. A violent order is disorder; and / B. A great disorder is an order"; or "There it was, word for word, / The poem that took the place of a mountain"? In addition, Stevens often employs strange characters, such as the mountain-minded Hoon, Professor Eucalyptus, and Canon Aspirin. He seldom uses the first-person form in his poetry, and when he does, it is likely to be in the plural form of "we." Although he occasionally chooses the second-person "you," he usually resorts to an anonymous third-person "he" or "she," or to the even more remote "one."

How then do we explain Stevens's subject and elucidate his greatness as a poet? The answer is simple: His major achievement is the expression of the self in all its amplitude and, in fact, teasingly beyond it. In this respect, he writes in the grand tradition of romantic poetry.

Ironically, his strategies of distancing—his use of odd characters, his opening philosophical gambits, his impersonal voice—serve to objectify and make authentic deeply personal sources of feeling and thought. To borrow Eliot's phrase, Stevens's poems become objective correlatives of various states within the reader, not only of heart and mind but also of being.

By analogy, consider what happens when one reads a poem such as Walt Whitman's "Song of Myself." Given the title, one naturally assumes that this is Whitman's personal declaration, his own song. After all, he begins rather explicitly: "I celebrate myself, and sing myself." But as one continues to read—as one absorbs the language, the sounds, the images, the rhythms—a revelation emerges. This is not Whitman's song of self at all, but rather "mine." Whitman's song of self has subtly transformed itself into the reader's. One realizes, sometimes with a jolt, that the title, "Song of Myself," is a play on words: it has a double and much more personal meaning.

Similarly, when Stevens writes, "And for what, except for you, do I feel love?" we, as readers, respond to the language, to our "need for words to express our thoughts and feelings." We search their sound "for a finality, a perfection, an unalterable vibration" that expresses not Stevens's self but ours. It is we who "press the extremest book of the wisest man / Close to [us], hidden in [us] day and night"; it is we who "sit at rest, / For a moment in the central of our being"; and it is we who discover that the "vivid transparence that [poetry brings] is peace." We are like the invisible audience in Stevens's "Of Modern Poetry" that listens "Not to the play, but to itself, expressed / In an emotion as of two people, as of two / Emotions becoming one." The poet, the "metaphysician in the dark," has created the music that gives "Sounds passing through sudden rightnesses." Stevens touches and moves our deepest and most private sense of self. In doing so, he fulfills his goal of making his imagination ours.

2

Such an observation about how Stevens's poetry works may seem to state the obvious, but too often this aspect of his work has been neglected. Criticism on Stevens is filled with erudite scholarship. It explores his philosophical perspectives, his sophisticated aesthetic theory, his relationship to other poets and to the other arts. There is even a book that criticizes Stevens for his lack of interpersonal relationships. But the true force of Stevens's poetry, what keeps drawing us back to his poems—to his words and images and metaphors and rhythms—is that he speaks to our vast and inarticulate interior world. Although his poems might have their sources in his personal reaction to the world—he once observed, "Poetry is a response to the daily necessity of getting the world right" (913)—they give voice to our own unique, personal, and otherwise tangled inner life.

Only a handful of readers, Helen Vendler and Harold Bloom most prominently, have emphasized this quality. Vendler elucidates the deeply private sources of Stevens's poetry, noting their roots in personal disappointment, in thwarted desire, and in a profound and brutal misery. She suggests that to read Stevens's poems "without a personal calibration . . . is to read them emptily."[3] Her useful tip, one that can assist a novice reader's approach to Stevens, is straightforward—"substitute 'I' whenever Stevens says 'he' or 'she': for 'Divinity must live within herself,' read 'Divinity must live within myself,' and so on" (44). Bloom places Stevens squarely "in the curiously esoteric but centrally American tradition of Emerson, Whitman, Thoreau and Dickinson."[4] He sees Stevens as the twentieth-century poet who best expresses "that solitary and inward glory we can none of us share with others":

> His value is that he describes and even celebrates (occasionally) our selfhood-communings as no one else can or does. He knows that "the sublime comes down / To the spirit and space," and though he keeps acknowledging the spirit's emptiness and space's vacancy, he keeps demonstrating a violent abundance of spirit and a florabundance of the consolations of space. He is the poet we always needed, who would speak for the solitude at our center, who would do for us what his own "Large Red Man Reading" did for those ghosts that returned to earth to hear his phrases, "and spoke the feeling for them, which was what they had lacked." (5)

Stevens's poems do more than that, too. By shaping these feelings, by giving them expressible form, they expand our sensibility, teaching us how to feel. Stevens's poetry becomes, as all art does, a two-way street. As the corresponding symbol of the inner life, his poems not only give shape and expression to our interior world, but in doing so, they also lend emotional import and expressiveness to the outer world. Stevens notes this effect in one of his essays, when he observes how a different description of a familiar place—such as Wordsworth's "This City now doth, like a garment, wear / The beauty of the morning, silent, bare"—invests reality with depth and human value. "This illustration must serve for all the rest," he says. "There is, in fact, a world of poetry indistinguishable from the world in which we live" (662). "The result," says the philosopher Susanne Langer, in speaking about the cultural value of the arts, "is an impregnation of ordinary reality with the significance of created form." Stevens's poetry, to modify Langer's terms slightly, objectifies subjective reality and subjectifies the outer experience of the world.[5]

3

Not all of Stevens's poems, of course, are so serious. Among the modernist poets, he is surely the funniest, wittiest, and most playful. His poetry is full of surprises, nonsense sounds, and a precise diction that frequently clashes and clangs. "Tum-ti-tum, / Ti-tum-tum-tum!" he blares in "Ploughing on Sunday," as he breaks the ground of the Fourth Commandment. "The Comedian as the Letter C" is a tour de force on the various hard and soft sounds of the letter *C*: "the quotidian / Like this, saps like the sun, true fortuner. / For all it takes it gives a humped return / Exchequering from piebald fiscs unkeyed." (In one of his letters, Stevens says, "The word exchequering is about as full of the sounds of C as any word that I can think of.")[6] And has there ever been a more lascivious description of a banana tree, one that simply exudes sexuality, than the one contained in Stevens's "Floral Decorations for Bananas"?

> And deck the bananas in leaves
> Plucked from the Carib trees,
> Fibrous and dangling down,

Oozing cantankerous gum
Out of their purple maws,
Darting out of their purple craws
Their musky and tingling tongues.

This flair for trumpeting language and a contagious joie de vivre flows throughout his poetry, from the early "Chieftain Iffucan of Azcan in caftan / Of tan with henna hackles, halt!" in "Bantams in Pine-Woods" to the late "whirroos / And scintillant sizzlings such as children like" in "A Primitive Like an Orb."

In addition, many of Stevens's poems are theoretical studies that engage the mind more than the feelings. In "Anecdote of Men by the Thousand," for example, he begins with a puzzling idea: "The soul, he said, is composed / Of the external world." This does not make much sense until he clarifies it with a tantalizing image:

The dress of a woman of Lhassa,
In its place,
Is an invisible element of that place
Made visible.

Poems such as "Study of Two Pears" and "Add This to Rhetoric" treat the philosophical issue of perception and the artist's problem of realization: "It is posed and it is posed. / But in nature it merely grows." Some longer poems, such as "Description Without Place," extend these questions by examining them from several angles. Exploring the notion that "we live in the description of a place and not in the place itself, and in every vital sense we do" (*Letters* 494), Stevens elaborates on an old theme: the idealist belief that reality exists in the mind. He posits the sun as an example: "What it seems / It is and in such seeming all things are." What is true of the sun is true of every individual's sense of reality—"Things seen are things as seen" (902):

Things are as they seemed to Calvin or to Anne
Of England, to Pablo Neruda in Ceylon,

To Nietzsche in Basel, to Lenin by a lake.

It is not a far step from such an individual's construction of reality to an era's: "An age is a manner collected from a queen."[7] These poems may not move us emotionally, but they do spur us intellectually. They transform us into introspective voyagers, questioners of our beliefs and certitudes. They excite the mind, test our core response to the world outside us, and deepen our self-awareness.

But for the most part, Stevens writes lyric poetry, a genre that by its nature is given to expression of the self. One could cite numerous examples of such evocations of genuine feeling in Stevens: the irreverent humor in "A High-Toned Old Christian Woman"; the cosmic fear communicated in "Domination of Black"; the discovery of a self "more truly and more strange" in "Tea at the Palaz of Hoon"; the ferocious sense of longing for one's homeland in "A Dish of Peaches in Russia"; the celebration of earth's sufficiency ("Air is air. / Its vacancy glitters round us everywhere") in "Evening Without Angels"; the dignified stance toward the loss of a loved one in "Waving Adieu, Adieu, Adieu" ("In a world without heaven to follow, the stops / Would be endings, more poignant than partings, profounder"); the comforting solitude afforded the reader in "Final Soliloquy of the Interior Paramour"; the strength of love as will in "The World as Meditation"; the lashing torment at the absence of coherent feeling in "Chaos in Motion and Not in Motion"; the inexplicable moments of joy ("One's tootings at the weddings of the soul") in "The Sense of the Sleight-of-Hand Man." One could go on and on, but the point is clear: we read Stevens not so much for his famed "reality-imagination complex" (*Letters* 792) as for his expression of another complex—the extensive register of feeling between our heavens and our hells.

The most remarkable aspect of Stevens's poetry is that he occasionally extends this register beyond its human scope. This is a paradox, but it is Stevens's most distinctive achievement. In an age of disbelief or, what might be worse, one of indifference to questions of belief, Stevens adds a metaphysical dimension. In doing so, he does not imply anything religious, yet he goes beyond humanism. "The chief defect of humanism," he writes, "is that it concerns human beings. Between humanism and something else, it might be possible to create an acceptable fiction" (*Letters* 449). That fiction is poetry, which he defines as "the supreme fiction." Poetry is supreme because it shifts our orientation from a traditional object of belief, such as God, to its source—the creative, ever changing, infinitely renewable process of constructing a credible truth. Its reward is pleasure. "A force capable of bringing about fluctuations in reality in words free from mysticism," he writes, "is a force independent of one's desire to elevate it" (639–40).

Stevens's enhancements of the self extend in two directions, from freshening expansions to utter extinctions. In "A Rabbit as King of the Ghosts," for example, the rabbit is a metaphor of the self. As the night comes on and as the threatening cat of reality withdraws, the reader partakes in the liberating solitude the rabbit experiences: "The whole of the wideness of night is for you, / A self that touches all edges." In other poems, Stevens has the uncanny talent to evoke pure being. One thinks of "The Latest Freed Man" ("To be without a description of to be"), "The River of Rivers in Connecticut" ("The mere flowing of the water is a gayety"), or "Of Mere Being." In the latter poem, "A gold-feathered bird" sits in a palm tree "Beyond the last thought" and "Sings in the palm, without human meaning, / Without human feeling, a foreign song." Such a moment of pure, unadulterated identity with the world outside the self conveys total fulfillment, and "You know then that it is not the reason / That makes us happy or unhappy":

> The bird sings. Its feathers shine.
> The palm stands on the edge of space.
> The wind moves slowly in the branches.
> The bird's fire-fangled feathers dangle down.

There are also poems that convey the experience of annihilation, as in "The Snow Man" (in which the listener, "nothing himself, beholds / Nothing that is not there and the nothing that is"), or "The Course of a Particular" (in which the cry of the leaves "concerns no one at all," and "being part is an exertion that declines"), or "A Clear Day and No Memories" ("Today the air is clear of everything. / It has no knowledge except of nothingness"). For me, at least, these, too, unbind the self, releasing a Kantian *Ding an sich,* "the thing itself"—phrases Stevens himself uses—to evoke the unrepresentable: the world outside and independent of the structuring categories of the mind. Some readers see the experience of nothingness in "The Snow Man," for example, as exemplifying the out-of-body experience of enlightenment in Zen Buddhism, the moment of complete identity with the cosmos without any intervention by human consciousness. Stevens describes it in more modest terms: "I shall explain The Snow Man as an example of the necessity of identifying oneself with reality in order to understand it and enjoy it" (*Letters* 464).

Such experiences in his lyrics can also show Stevens to be among the most compassionate and personal of poets. In "Lebensweisheitspielerei" ("Playing Around with Words of Wisdom"), for example, he empathizes so profoundly with the ache of total human mortality that he reaches out to everyone. It is an extraordinary moment, one that has been achieved by few poets:

> Little by little, the poverty
> Of autumnal space becomes
> A look, a few words spoken.
>
> Each person completely touches us
> With what he is and as he is,
> In the stale grandeur of annihilation.

What are we to make, however, of the long, philosophical meditations such as "The Man with the Blue Guitar," "Esthétique du Mal," "Notes Toward a Supreme Fiction," "The Auroras of Autumn," or "An Ordinary Evening in New Haven"? These difficult poems demand an unusual amount of concentration. As poems of process, as poems of shifting perspective and movement, they absorb us totally, engaging us more deeply and more profoundly than briefer poems. They fulfill Stevens's definition of modern poetry as "The poem of the mind in the act of finding / What will suffice." Just as Charles Ives could "keep five, even six, rhythms going in [his] mind at once,"[8] these extended variations on a theme challenge us to contend with multiple and often contradictory ideas, feelings, and viewpoints. Yet each poem contains climactic moments that touch the very core of our being, moments that cannot be easily summarized or paraphrased. Nor do these moments last. But they erupt in a crescendo of feeling in virtually every long poem: "How should you walk in that space and know / Nothing of the madness of space" ("The Man with the Blue Guitar"); "And out of what one sees and hears and out / Of what one feels, who could have thought to make / So many selves, so many sensuous worlds" ("Esthétique du Mal"); "Is it I then that keep saying there is an hour / Filled with expressible bliss, in which I have / No need, am happy, forget need's golden hand" ("Notes Toward a Supreme Fiction"); "The scholar of one candle sees / An Arctic effulgence flaring on the frame / Of everything he is. And he feels afraid" ("The Auroras of Autumn"); "There was a clearing, a readiness for first bells . . . There was a willingness not yet composed . . . An escape from repetition, a happening / In space and the self, that touched them both at once / And alike" ("An Ordinary Evening in New Haven").

As a modernist poet, Stevens is wary of anything that smacks of the visionary or mystical. Consequently, he takes at the very moment that he gives. In "Credences of Summer," for example, after enriching the "stratagems / Of the spirit" by penetrating "the more than visible," he abruptly halts, and "A complex of emotions falls apart." With that, the ecstatic moment is gone. Stevens's use of qualifiers and provisional statements—"as if," "it is possible," "for a moment," "if only"—is legendary. But these rhetorical gestures constitute the transformative magic of his poetry, for it is these very disclaimers that serve to strengthen, to make more credible "that solitary and inward glory we can none of us share with others." As Stevens says in "A Primitive Like an Orb," "It is and it / Is not and, therefore, is."

4

Wallace Stevens was always more at home in the world of written rather than spoken language. His journals as a young man growing up in Reading, Pennsylvania, describe the subtlest observations of nature. Similarly, his letters to his fiancée, Elsie Kachel, over their five-year courtship contain delicate and tender expressions of love. After establishing himself as a lawyer at the Hartford Accident and Indemnity Company, where he headed the fidelity and surety claims department soon after his arrival in 1916 until his death in 1955, he maintained an extensive correspondence with people from around the world—art dealers and booksellers, editors, poets, philosophers, scholars, students, and friends. Most of this correspondence displays an intimate, respectful, and touching warmth. In certain social situations, he could be affable and generous. On his yearly excursions to Florida, for example, he loved to let himself go and be "one of the boys." He regularly attended the Harvard-Yale football games, which meant a weekend in Boston with colleagues. He assisted people financially and encouraged younger employees to better their education. Most of all, he enjoyed his frequent trips to New York, that "wild country of the soul" ("Arrival at the Waldorf"), where he could dine with friends, visit art galleries, and return home to await shipments of select wines and exotic fruits.

But in his day-to-day interaction with neighbors, colleagues, and business associates, he was often uneasy, curt, and sometimes rude. Peter Brazeau's oral biography contains numerous anecdotes that cast Stevens as a "superintellect," an industrious and dedicated worker ("the dean of surety-claims men in the whole country"),[9] but a man who preferred to work alone. Some colleagues revered him: "[H]e was a very lonesome man in many ways, and that's why he built his life around a half dozen of us pretty much. . . . That I broke down here shows my affection for him" (Brazeau 81). But most acquaintances found him aloof and condescending. One recalls: "He had difficulty relating to people. . . . He was not what I call a hail-fellow-well-met person. He could put away a good many martinis [at the Canoe Club in Hartford during his once-a-week lunch on Wednesday] and he would try to relax, but he didn't succeed very well" (Brazeau 27, 29). Another recalls a time when, on a whim, he directed a colleague to drive him to New York instead of the office. A gourmet, Stevens wanted to have lunch at the 1939 World's Fair. Yet, upon his arrival, he told his driver—a lawyer like himself—to get what he wanted and to return in an hour. On another occasion, a visit to an art gallery in New York, he advised his companion to "go someplace else. You wouldn't understand these things" (Brazeau 65). Sometimes his attempts at being witty were misconstrued, I believe, as satire. For example, at a social gathering the night before he was to receive an honorary degree, his host—either the president of the university or a trustee—asked Stevens what he thought of his house. Stevens responded, "My wife and I have tried very hard *not* to create this effect" (Brazeau 59).

His marriage to Elsie Kachel, "the most beautiful girl in Reading" (Brazeau 286), soured early on. Thereafter, he and his wife lived virtually separate lives, and they rarely entertained. In Hartford, Stevens lived monastically. He walked the two miles to and from the office during the week, composing poetry in his stride.[10] He strolled through his beloved Elizabeth Park near his home on weekends. Nightly, he retreated alone to his bedroom suite after supper. One of his assistants at the Hartford recollects: "I was one of the few persons that got inside the house. . . . He had a bedroom area that was furnished up like a library and a sitting room, and he spent most of his time in there, reading nights. . . . He had a load of books; he read almost all the time" (Brazeau 32).

Given the unhappiness of his domestic life, Stevens was most content when he was alone. Then he could inhabit his world of creation. In one of his essays, he speaks, rather hierophantically, about the "sense of liberation," the "state of elevation," that the poet experiences when "writing a poem that completely accomplishes [his] purpose" (673–4). In one of his letters, he cites a "precious sentence in Henry James" that clearly reflects his own experience:

> "To live *in* the world of creation—to get into it and stay in it—to frequent it and haunt it—to *think* intensely and fruitfully—to woo combinations and inspirations into being by a depth and continuity of attention and meditation—this is the only thing." (*Letters* 506)

Early scholars favored the view that Stevens lived two separate lives: that of the businessman and that of the poet. On one hand, much has been done to address this mistaken assumption. Stevens himself remarked that he was the same person when either handling law cases or writing poetry, and he found it "odd that people should think business and poetry incompatible" (*Letters* 612). There are telling anecdotes about Stevens at work, dictating a letter to his secretary and stopping, "right in the middle of dictating," and reaching down for his pad to write a line or two of poetry (Brazeau 38). On the other hand, we must not forget that Stevens was a poetic genius. His talents as a lawyer, where reason and logic prevailed, were not the same as those that flowed from his poetic impulse. Although he was well aware of the poet's role as a maker and that poems were shaped by "an effort of the mind" (744), he also acknowledged that they stemmed from the constructive faculty of the "imagination or by the miraculous kind of reason that the imagination sometimes promotes" (744). In other words, his poems often had sources beyond the rational and sometimes surpassed even his own cognitive understanding. This is no doubt why he comments, no fewer than three times in his essays, that poets are born and not made (717, 782, 819).

On one occasion, the music composer John Gruen asked Stevens how he wrote poetry. Stevens was quite vague in his answer, says Gruen; it was such a personal matter that he had difficulty speaking about it:

> He spoke more about the experience of how it is to make a poem. He told me that he didn't know what his poetry meant at times, that he really had to think hard as to what he meant by that image or that phrase or that word, even. He talked something about submersion, about words being submerged and then rising out, that they seemed to have been hidden and then revealed themselves. . . . There was something rather mysterious about his writing the poetry. (Brazeau 207)

This is the very process Stevens describes in his poem "The Creations of Sound," in which "there are words / Better without an author, without a poet. / . . . We say ourselves in syllables that rise / From the floor, rising in speech we do not speak." In other words, Stevens's poetic gift to express humanity through his art, although it might have derived from his personal response to the world, his idiosyncratic sensibility, is never mere self-expression. "Poetry is not personal" (902), he notes. Like all genuine art, it is universal.

In 1948, when he was sixty-eight, Stevens traveled to New York to meet with José Rodríguez Feo, a young Cuban poet and editor, whom Stevens had befriended several years earlier and with whom he had been corresponding. On this occasion, Rodríguez Feo recalls, both got drunk. To provoke him, Rodríguez Feo asked Stevens point-blank whether he thought he was a great poet. "Well, we've had a few drinks," responded Stevens, "and when you have a few drinks you can say a lot of silly things: but I think that if I'm not a great poet I'm getting pretty near to being a great poet." That, Rodríguez Feo notes, was the first time he had ever heard Stevens boast about anything. Then he asked, "Why do you think you're a great poet?" Stevens responded, "I don't know why I think I'm a great poet, but I'm beginning to write great poetry" (Brazeau 144). No one could have said it better, drunk or sober.

In the early 1950s, when Stevens was in his early seventies, Alfred A. Knopf approached him about doing either a selected or a collected volume. Giving some thought to the end of his poetic career, Stevens indicated he would like to celebrate the occasion of his seventy-fifth birthday, which would be on October 2, 1954, with "a selected volume as against a collected volume" (*Letters* 759). By the time his birthday neared, however, he had changed his mind. In a letter to an acquaintance on April 27, 1954, he commented, "A collection is very much like sweeping under the rug. As for a selection, I always thought that someone else should make it. But the question has come up again. I had written to [Knopf] to say that I was content to have a collection published" (*Letters* 829). Then he added:

I have no particular objection to a selection against a collection. They are different in the sense that people read selected poems but don't buy them. On the other hand, they buy collected poems but don't read them. (*Letters* 829)

As an example of Stevens's wit, this is endearing. But it is also comforting to note that we have proven him wrong on one count and, in time, I hope, we will prove him wrong on both. His *Collected Poems* has become one of the most widely read volumes of any twentieth-century American poet. My wish is that this slimmer volume of selected poems will also become a prized possession, one that readers will keep close, hidden in them day and night, so that they might cherish, in the central of their being, the vivid transparence that his poetry brings.

John N. Serio
Clarkson University

NOTES

1 Wallace Stevens, *Wallace Stevens: Collected Poetry and Prose,* ed. Frank Kermode and Joan Richardson (New York: Library of America, 1997), 662–3. Further quotations from this source will be cited parenthetically in the text with page number only.

2 T. S. Eliot, "The Love Song of J. Alfred Prufrock," *T. S. Eliot: Collected Poems: 1909–1962* (New York: Harcourt, Brace & World, Inc., 1963), 3.

3 Helen Vendler, *Words Chosen Out of Desire* (Knoxville: University of Tennessee Press, 1984), 8.

4 Harold Bloom, Introduction, *Wallace Stevens,* ed. Harold Bloom (New York: Chelsea House Publishers, 1985), 5.

5 Susanne K. Langer, "The Cultural Importance of the Arts," *Journal of Aesthetic Education* 1.1 (Spring 1966): 5–12. Langer concludes her discussion with the following: "The arts objectify subjective reality, and subjectify outward experience of nature" (12).

6 Wallace Stevens, *Letters of Wallace Stevens,* ed. Holly Stevens (New York: Knopf, 1966), 352.

7 In discussing the influence of the arts on human life, Langer notes:

As language actually gives form to our sense-experience, grouping our impressions around those things which have names, and fitting sensations to the qualities that have adjectival names, and so on, the arts we live with—our picture books and stories and the music we hear—actually form our emotive experience. Every generation has its styles of feeling. One age shudders and blushes and faints, another swaggers, still another is godlike in a universal indifference. These styles in actual emotions are not insincere. They are largely unconscious—determined by many social causes, but *shaped* by artists. . . . [O]ur emotions are largely Shakespeare's poetry. (11)

8 Charles Ives, *Memos,* ed. John Kirkpatrick (New York: W. W. Norton, 1972), 125.

9 Peter Brazeau, *Parts of a World: Wallace Stevens Remembered; An Oral Biography* (New York: Random House, 1983), 14, 67.

10　Stevens frequently composed poetry during these walks. In a letter of September 20, 1954, he described his method of composition:

> I have no set way of working. A great deal of my poetry has been written while I have been out walking. Walking helps me to concentrate and I suppose that, somehow or other, my own movement gets into the movement of the poems. I have to jot things down as I go along since, otherwise, by the time I got to the end of the poem I should have forgotten the beginning. Often, when I reach the office, I hand my notes to my stenographer who does a better job frequently at deciphering them than I should be able to do myself. Then I pull and tug at the typed script until I have the thing the way I want it, when I put it away for a week or two until I have forgotten about it and can take it up as if it was something entirely fresh. If it satisfies me at that time, that is the end of it. (*Letters* 844)

A NOTE ON THE TEXT

Wallace Stevens frequently used the British spelling for words such as "marvellous," "labelled," "sombre," "meagre," and "lustre." Since these occurrences do not vary in his published poetry, they have been retained in this selection. The spelling of "centre" vs. "center," however, has a mixed publication history and appears in both forms. When his publisher queried him about this discrepancy in *The Auroras of Autumn*, Stevens responded:

> Center is correct. One of the principal streets in the place where I came from is called Centre Avenue. I have never quite been able to shake that off. (Letter to Herbert Weinstock, Alfred A. Knopf, Inc., January 27, 1950)

For consistency, the American spelling of "center" has been adopted throughout. Several typographical, punctuation, and formatting errors have been corrected.

Selected Poems

EARTHY ANECDOTE

Every time the bucks went clattering
Over Oklahoma
A firecat bristled in the way.

Wherever they went,
They went clattering,
Until they swerved
In a swift, circular line
To the right,
Because of the firecat.

Or until they swerved
In a swift, circular line
To the left,
Because of the firecat.

The bucks clattered.
The firecat went leaping,
To the right, to the left,
And
Bristled in the way.

Later, the firecat closed his bright eyes
And slept.

THE PALTRY NUDE STARTS ON A SPRING VOYAGE

But not on a shell, she starts,
Archaic, for the sea.
But on the first-found weed
She scuds the glitters,
Noiselessly, like one more wave.

She too is discontent
And would have purple stuff upon her arms,
Tired of the salty harbors,
Eager for the brine and bellowing
Of the high interiors of the sea.

The wind speeds her,
Blowing upon her hands
And watery back.
She touches the clouds, where she goes
In the circle of her traverse of the sea.

Yet this is meagre play
In the scurry and water-shine,
As her heels foam—
Not as when the goldener nude
Of a later day

Will go, like the center of sea-green pomp,
In an intenser calm,
Scullion of fate,
Across the spick torrent, ceaselessly,
Upon her irretrievable way.

THE PLOT AGAINST THE GIANT

FIRST GIRL

When this yokel comes maundering,
Whetting his hacker,
I shall run before him,
Diffusing the civilest odors
Out of geraniums and unsmelled flowers.
It will check him.

SECOND GIRL

I shall run before him,
Arching cloths besprinkled with colors
As small as fish-eggs.
The threads
Will abash him.

THIRD GIRL

Oh, la . . . le pauvre!
I shall run before him,
With a curious puffing.
He will bend his ear then.
I shall whisper
Heavenly labials in a world of gutturals.
It will undo him.

DOMINATION OF BLACK

At night, by the fire,
The colors of the bushes
And of the fallen leaves,
Repeating themselves,
Turned in the room,
Like the leaves themselves
Turning in the wind.
Yes: but the color of the heavy hemlocks
Came striding.
And I remembered the cry of the peacocks.

The colors of their tails
Were like the leaves themselves
Turning in the wind,
In the twilight wind.
They swept over the room,
Just as they flew from the boughs of the hemlocks
Down to the ground.
I heard them cry—the peacocks.
Was it a cry against the twilight
Or against the leaves themselves
Turning in the wind,
Turning as the flames
Turned in the fire,
Turning as the tails of the peacocks
Turned in the loud fire,
Loud as the hemlocks
Full of the cry of the peacocks?
Or was it a cry against the hemlocks?

Out of the window,
I saw how the planets gathered
Like the leaves themselves
Turning in the wind.
I saw how the night came,
Came striding like the color of the heavy hemlocks.
I felt afraid.
And I remembered the cry of the peacocks.

THE SNOW MAN

One must have a mind of winter
To regard the frost and the boughs
Of the pine-trees crusted with snow;

And have been cold a long time
To behold the junipers shagged with ice,
The spruces rough in the distant glitter

Of the January sun; and not to think
Of any misery in the sound of the wind,
In the sound of a few leaves,

Which is the sound of the land
Full of the same wind
That is blowing in the same bare place

For the listener, who listens in the snow,
And, nothing himself, beholds
Nothing that is not there and the nothing that is.

LE MONOCLE DE MON ONCLE

I

"Mother of heaven, regina of the clouds,
O sceptre of the sun, crown of the moon,
There is not nothing, no, no, never nothing,
Like the clashed edges of two words that kill."
And so I mocked her in magnificent measure.
Or was it that I mocked myself alone?
I wish that I might be a thinking stone.
The sea of spuming thought foists up again
The radiant bubble that she was. And then
A deep up-pouring from some saltier well
Within me, bursts its watery syllable.

II

A red bird flies across the golden floor.
It is a red bird that seeks out his choir
Among the choirs of wind and wet and wing.
A torrent will fall from him when he finds.
Shall I uncrumple this much-crumpled thing?
I am a man of fortune greeting heirs;
For it has come that thus I greet the spring.
These choirs of welcome choir for me farewell.
No spring can follow past meridian.
Yet you persist with anecdotal bliss
To make believe a starry *connaissance.*

III

Is it for nothing, then, that old Chinese
Sat tittivating by their mountain pools
Or in the Yangtse studied out their beards?
I shall not play the flat historic scale.
You know how Utamaro's beauties sought
The end of love in their all-speaking braids.
You know the mountainous coiffures of Bath.

Alas! Have all the barbers lived in vain
That not one curl in nature has survived?
Why, without pity on these studious ghosts,
Do you come dripping in your hair from sleep?

IV

This luscious and impeccable fruit of life
Falls, it appears, of its own weight to earth.
When you were Eve, its acrid juice was sweet,
Untasted, in its heavenly, orchard air.
An apple serves as well as any skull
To be the book in which to read a round,
And is as excellent, in that it is composed
Of what, like skulls, comes rotting back to ground.
But it excels in this, that as the fruit
Of love, it is a book too mad to read
Before one merely reads to pass the time.

V

In the high west there burns a furious star.
It is for fiery boys that star was set
And for sweet-smelling virgins close to them.
The measure of the intensity of love
Is measure, also, of the verve of earth.
For me, the firefly's quick, electric stroke
Ticks tediously the time of one more year.
And you? Remember how the crickets came
Out of their mother grass, like little kin,
In the pale nights, when your first imagery
Found inklings of your bond to all that dust.

VI

If men at forty will be painting lakes
The ephemeral blues must merge for them in one,
The basic slate, the universal hue.

There is a substance in us that prevails.
But in our amours amorists discern
Such fluctuations that their scrivening
Is breathless to attend each quirky turn.
When amorists grow bald, then amours shrink
Into the compass and curriculum
Of introspective exiles, lecturing.
It is a theme for Hyacinth alone.

VII

The mules that angels ride come slowly down
The blazing passes, from beyond the sun.
Descensions of their tinkling bells arrive.
These muleteers are dainty of their way.
Meantime, centurions guffaw and beat
Their shrilling tankards on the table-boards.
This parable, in sense, amounts to this:
The honey of heaven may or may not come,
But that of earth both comes and goes at once.
Suppose these couriers brought amid their train
A damsel heightened by eternal bloom.

VIII

Like a dull scholar, I behold, in love,
An ancient aspect touching a new mind.
It comes, it blooms, it bears its fruit and dies.
This trivial trope reveals a way of truth.
Our bloom is gone. We are the fruit thereof.
Two golden gourds distended on our vines,
We hang like warty squashes, streaked and rayed,
Into the autumn weather, splashed with frost,
Distorted by hale fatness, turned grotesque.
The laughing sky will see the two of us
Washed into rinds by rotting winter rains.

IX

In verses wild with motion, full of din,
Loudened by cries, by clashes, quick and sure
As the deadly thought of men accomplishing
Their curious fates in war, come, celebrate
The faith of forty, ward of Cupido.
Most venerable heart, the lustiest conceit
Is not too lusty for your broadening.
I quiz all sounds, all thoughts, all everything
For the music and manner of the paladins
To make oblation fit. Where shall I find
Bravura adequate to this great hymn?

X

The fops of fancy in their poems leave
Memorabilia of the mystic spouts,
Spontaneously watering their gritty soils.
I am a yeoman, as such fellows go.
I know no magic trees, no balmy boughs,
No silver-ruddy, gold-vermilion fruits.
But, after all, I know a tree that bears
A semblance to the thing I have in mind.
It stands gigantic, with a certain tip
To which all birds come sometime in their time.
But when they go that tip still tips the tree.

XI

If sex were all, then every trembling hand
Could make us squeak, like dolls, the wished-for words.
But note the unconscionable treachery of fate,
That makes us weep, laugh, grunt and groan, and shout
Doleful heroics, pinching gestures forth
From madness or delight, without regard
To that first, foremost law. Anguishing hour!

Last night, we sat beside a pool of pink,
Clippered with lilies scudding the bright chromes,
Keen to the point of starlight, while a frog
Boomed from his very belly odious chords.

XII

A blue pigeon it is, that circles the blue sky,
On sidelong wing, around and round and round.
A white pigeon it is, that flutters to the ground,
Grown tired of flight. Like a dark rabbi, I
Observed, when young, the nature of mankind,
In lordly study. Every day, I found
Man proved a gobbet in my mincing world.
Like a rose rabbi, later, I pursued,
And still pursue, the origin and course
Of love, but until now I never knew
That fluttering things have so distinct a shade.

NUANCES OF A THEME BY WILLIAMS

It's a strange courage
you give me, ancient star:

Shine alone in the sunrise
toward which you lend no part!

I

Shine alone, shine nakedly, shine like bronze,
that reflects neither my face nor any inner part
of my being, shine like fire, that mirrors nothing.

II

Lend no part to any humanity that suffuses
you in its own light.
Be not chimera of morning,
Half-man, half-star.
Be not an intelligence,
Like a widow's bird
Or an old horse.

PLOUGHING ON SUNDAY

The white cock's tail
Tosses in the wind.
The turkey-cock's tail
Glitters in the sun.

Water in the fields.
The wind pours down.
The feathers flare
And bluster in the wind.

Remus, blow your horn!
I'm ploughing on Sunday,
Ploughing North America.
Blow your horn!

Tum-ti-tum,
Ti-tum-tum-tum!
The turkey-cock's tail
Spreads to the sun.

The white cock's tail
Streams to the moon.
Water in the fields.
The wind pours down.

CY EST POURTRAICTE, MADAME STE URSULE, ET LES UNZE MILLE VIERGES

Ursula, in a garden, found
A bed of radishes.
She kneeled upon the ground
And gathered them,
With flowers around,
Blue, gold, pink, and green.

She dressed in red and gold brocade
And in the grass an offering made
Of radishes and flowers.

She said, "My dear,
Upon your altars,
I have placed
The marguerite and coquelicot,
And roses
Frail as April snow;
But here," she said,
"Where none can see,
I make an offering, in the grass,
Of radishes and flowers."
And then she wept
For fear the Lord would not accept.

The good Lord in His garden sought
New leaf and shadowy tinct,
And they were all His thought.
He heard her low accord,
Half prayer and half ditty,
And He felt a subtle quiver,
That was not heavenly love,
Or pity.

This is not writ
In any book.

THE DOCTOR OF GENEVA

The doctor of Geneva stamped the sand
That lay impounding the Pacific swell,
Patted his stove-pipe hat and tugged his shawl.

Lacustrine man had never been assailed
By such long-rolling opulent cataracts,
Unless Racine or Bossuet held the like.

He did not quail. A man so used to plumb
The multifarious heavens felt no awe
Before these visible, voluble delugings,

Which yet found means to set his simmering mind
Spinning and hissing with oracular
Notations of the wild, the ruinous waste,

Until the steeples of his city clanked and sprang
In an unburgherly apocalypse.
The doctor used his handkerchief and sighed.

THE COMEDIAN AS THE LETTER C

THE WORLD WITHOUT IMAGINATION

Nota: man is the intelligence of his soil,
The sovereign ghost. As such, the Socrates
Of snails, musician of pears, principium
And lex. Sed quaeritur: is this same wig
Of things, this nincompated pedagogue,
Preceptor to the sea? Crispin at sea
Created, in his day, a touch of doubt.
An eye most apt in gelatines and jupes,
Berries of villages, a barber's eye,
An eye of land, of simple salad-beds,
Of honest quilts, the eye of Crispin, hung
On porpoises, instead of apricots,
And on silentious porpoises, whose snouts
Dibbled in waves that were mustachios,
Inscrutable hair in an inscrutable world.

One eats one paté, even of salt, quotha.
It was not so much the lost terrestrial,
The snug hibernal from that sea and salt,
That century of wind in a single puff.
What counted was mythology of self,
Blotched out beyond unblotching. Crispin,
The lutanist of fleas, the knave, the thane,
The ribboned stick, the bellowing breeches, cloak
Of China, cap of Spain, imperative haw
Of hum, inquisitorial botanist,
And general lexicographer of mute
And maidenly greenhorns, now beheld himself,
A skinny sailor peering in the sea-glass.
What word split up in clickering syllables
And storming under multitudinous tones
Was name for this short-shanks in all that brunt?
Crispin was washed away by magnitude.
The whole of life that still remained in him
Dwindled to one sound strumming in his ear,
Ubiquitous concussion, slap and sigh,
Polyphony beyond his baton's thrust.

Could Crispin stem verboseness in the sea,
The old age of a watery realist,
Triton, dissolved in shifting diaphanes
Of blue and green? A wordy, watery age
That whispered to the sun's compassion, made
A convocation, nightly, of the sea-stars,
And on the clopping foot-ways of the moon
Lay grovelling. Triton incomplicate with that
Which made him Triton, nothing left of him,
Except in faint, memorial gesturings,
That were like arms and shoulders in the waves,
Here, something in the rise and fall of wind
That seemed hallucinating horn, and here,
A sunken voice, both of remembering
And of forgetfulness, in alternate strain.
Just so an ancient Crispin was dissolved.
The valet in the tempest was annulled.
Bordeaux to Yucatan, Havana next,
And then to Carolina. Simple jaunt.
Crispin, merest minuscule in the gales,
Dejected his manner to the turbulence.
The salt hung on his spirit like a frost,
The dead brine melted in him like a dew
Of winter, until nothing of himself
Remained, except some starker, barer self
In a starker, barer world, in which the sun
Was not the sun because it never shone
With bland complaisance on pale parasols,
Beetled, in chapels, on the chaste bouquets.
Against his pipping sounds a trumpet cried
Celestial sneering boisterously. Crispin
Became an introspective voyager.

Here was the veritable ding an sich, at last,
Crispin confronting it, a vocable thing,
But with a speech belched out of hoary darks
Noway resembling his, a visible thing,

And excepting negligible Triton, free
From the unavoidable shadow of himself
That lay elsewhere around him. Severance
Was clear. The last distortion of romance
Forsook the insatiable egotist. The sea
Severs not only lands but also selves.
Here was no help before reality.
Crispin beheld and Crispin was made new.
The imagination, here, could not evade,
In poems of plums, the strict austerity
Of one vast, subjugating, final tone.
The drenching of stale lives no more fell down.
What was this gaudy, gusty panoply?
Out of what swift destruction did it spring?
It was caparison of wind and cloud
And something given to make whole among
The ruses that were shattered by the large.

II

CONCERNING THE THUNDERSTORMS OF YUCATAN

In Yucatan, the Maya sonneteers
Of the Caribbean amphitheatre,
In spite of hawk and falcon, green toucan
And jay, still to the night-bird made their plea,
As if raspberry tanagers in palms,
High up in orange air, were barbarous.
But Crispin was too destitute to find
In any commonplace the sought-for aid.
He was a man made vivid by the sea,
A man come out of luminous traversing,
Much trumpeted, made desperately clear,
Fresh from discoveries of tidal skies,
To whom oracular rockings gave no rest.
Into a savage color he went on.

How greatly had he grown in his demesne,
This auditor of insects! He that saw
The stride of vanishing autumn in a park
By way of decorous melancholy; he
That wrote his couplet yearly to the spring,
As dissertation of profound delight,
Stopping, on voyage, in a land of snakes,
Found his vicissitudes had much enlarged
His apprehension, made him intricate
In moody rucks, and difficult and strange
In all desires, his destitution's mark.
He was in this as other freemen are,
Sonorous nutshells rattling inwardly.
His violence was for aggrandizement
And not for stupor, such as music makes
For sleepers halfway waking. He perceived
That coolness for his heat came suddenly,
And only, in the fables that he scrawled
With his own quill, in its indigenous dew,
Of an aesthetic tough, diverse, untamed,
Incredible to prudes, the mint of dirt,
Green barbarism turning paradigm.
Crispin foresaw a curious promenade
Or, nobler, sensed an elemental fate,
And elemental potencies and pangs,
And beautiful barenesses as yet unseen,
Making the most of savagery of palms,
Of moonlight on the thick, cadaverous bloom
That yuccas breed, and of the panther's tread.
The fabulous and its intrinsic verse
Came like two spirits parleying, adorned
In radiance from the Atlantic coign,
For Crispin and his quill to catechize.
But they came parleying of such an earth,
So thick with sides and jagged lops of green,
So intertwined with serpent-kin encoiled

Among the purple tufts, the scarlet crowns,
Scenting the jungle in their refuges,
So streaked with yellow, blue and green and red
In beak and bud and fruity gobbet-skins,
That earth was like a jostling festival
Of seeds grown fat, too juicily opulent,
Expanding in the gold's maternal warmth.

So much for that. The affectionate emigrant found
A new reality in parrot-squawks.
Yet let that trifle pass. Now, as this odd
Discoverer walked through the harbor streets
Inspecting the cabildo, the façade
Of the cathedral, making notes, he heard
A rumbling, west of Mexico, it seemed,
Approaching like a gasconade of drums.
The white cabildo darkened, the façade,
As sullen as the sky, was swallowed up
In swift, successive shadows, dolefully.
The rumbling broadened as it fell. The wind,
Tempestuous clarion, with heavy cry,
Came bluntly thundering, more terrible
Than the revenge of music on bassoons.
Gesticulating lightning, mystical,
Made pallid flitter. Crispin, here, took flight.
An annotator has his scruples, too.
He knelt in the cathedral with the rest,
This connoisseur of elemental fate,
Aware of exquisite thought. The storm was one
Of many proclamations of the kind,
Proclaiming something harsher than he learned
From hearing signboards whimper in cold nights
Or seeing the midsummer artifice
Of heat upon his pane. This was the span
Of force, the quintessential fact, the note
Of Vulcan, that a valet seeks to own,
The thing that makes him envious in phrase.

And while the torrent on the roof still droned
He felt the Andean breath. His mind was free
And more than free, elate, intent, profound
And studious of a self possessing him,
That was not in him in the crusty town
From which he sailed. Beyond him, westward, lay
The mountainous ridges, purple balustrades,
In which the thunder, lapsing in its clap,
Let down gigantic quavers of its voice,
For Crispin to vociferate again.

III

APPROACHING CAROLINA

The book of moonlight is not written yet
Nor half begun, but, when it is, leave room
For Crispin, fagot in the lunar fire,
Who, in the hubbub of his pilgrimage
Through sweating changes, never could forget
That wakefulness or meditating sleep,
In which the sulky strophes willingly
Bore up, in time, the somnolent, deep songs.
Leave room, therefore, in that unwritten book
For the legendary moonlight that once burned
In Crispin's mind above a continent.
America was always north to him,
A northern west or western north, but north,
And thereby polar, polar-purple, chilled
And lank, rising and slumping from a sea
Of hardy foam, receding flatly, spread
In endless ledges, glittering, submerged
And cold in a boreal mistiness of the moon.
The spring came there in clinking pannicles
Of half-dissolving frost, the summer came,
If ever, whisked and wet, not ripening,

Before the winter's vacancy returned.
The myrtle, if the myrtle ever bloomed,
Was like a glacial pink upon the air.
The green palmettoes in crepuscular ice
Clipped frigidly blue-black meridians,
Morose chiaroscuro, gauntly drawn.

How many poems he denied himself
In his observant progress, lesser things
Than the relentless contact he desired;
How many sea-masks he ignored; what sounds
He shut out from his tempering ear; what thoughts,
Like jades affecting the sequestered bride;
And what descants, he sent to banishment!
Perhaps the Arctic moonlight really gave
The liaison, the blissful liaison,
Between himself and his environment,
Which was, and is, chief motive, first delight,
For him, and not for him alone. It seemed
Illusive, faint, more mist than moon, perverse,
Wrong as a divagation to Peking,
To him that postulated as his theme
The vulgar, as his theme and hymn and flight,
A passionately niggling nightingale.
Moonlight was an evasion, or, if not,
A minor meeting, facile, delicate.

Thus he conceived his voyaging to be
An up and down between two elements,
A fluctuating between sun and moon,
A sally into gold and crimson forms,
As on this voyage, out of goblinry,
And then retirement like a turning back
And sinking down to the indulgences
That in the moonlight have their habitude.
But let these backward lapses, if they would,
Grind their seductions on him, Crispin knew

It was a flourishing tropic he required
For his refreshment, an abundant zone,
Prickly and obdurate, dense, harmonious
Yet with a harmony not rarefied
Nor fined for the inhibited instruments
Of over-civil stops. And thus he tossed
Between a Carolina of old time,
A little juvenile, an ancient whim,
And the visible, circumspect presentment drawn
From what he saw across his vessel's prow.

He came. The poetic hero without palms
Or jugglery, without regalia.
And as he came he saw that it was spring,
A time abhorrent to the nihilist
Or searcher for the fecund minimum.
The moonlight fiction disappeared. The spring,
Although contending featly in its veils,
Irised in dew and early fragrancies,
Was gemmy marionette to him that sought
A sinewy nakedness. A river bore
The vessel inward. Tilting up his nose,
He inhaled the rancid rosin, burly smells
Of dampened lumber, emanations blown
From warehouse doors, the gustiness of ropes,
Decays of sacks, and all the arrant stinks
That helped him round his rude aesthetic out.
He savored rankness like a sensualist.
He marked the marshy ground around the dock,
The crawling railroad spur, the rotten fence,
Curriculum for the marvellous sophomore.
It purified. It made him see how much
Of what he saw he never saw at all.
He gripped more closely the essential prose
As being, in a world so falsified,

The one integrity for him, the one
Discovery still possible to make,
To which all poems were incident, unless
That prose should wear a poem's guise at last.

IV

THE IDEA OF A COLONY

Nota: his soil is man's intelligence.
That's better. That's worth crossing seas to find.
Crispin in one laconic phrase laid bare
His cloudy drift and planned a colony.
Exit the mental moonlight, exit lex,
Rex and principium, exit the whole
Shebang. Exeunt omnes. Here was prose
More exquisite than any tumbling verse:
A still new continent in which to dwell.
What was the purpose of his pilgrimage,
Whatever shape it took in Crispin's mind,
If not, when all is said, to drive away
The shadow of his fellows from the skies,
And, from their stale intelligence released,
To make a new intelligence prevail?
Hence the reverberations in the words
Of his first central hymns, the celebrants
Of rankest trivia, tests of the strength
Of his aesthetic, his philosophy,
The more invidious, the more desired:
The florist asking aid from cabbages,
The rich man going bare, the paladin
Afraid, the blind man as astronomer,
The appointed power unwielded from disdain.
His western voyage ended and began.
The torment of fastidious thought grew slack,
Another, still more bellicose, came on.

He, therefore, wrote his prolegomena,
And, being full of the caprice, inscribed
Commingled souvenirs and prophecies.
He made a singular collation. Thus:
The natives of the rain are rainy men.
Although they paint effulgent, azure lakes,
And April hillsides wooded white and pink,
Their azure has a cloudy edge, their white
And pink, the water bright that dogwood bears.
And in their music showering sounds intone.
On what strange froth does the gross Indian dote,
What Eden sapling gum, what honeyed gore,
What pulpy dram distilled of innocence,
That streaking gold should speak in him
Or bask within his images and words?
If these rude instances impeach themselves
By force of rudeness, let the principle
Be plain. For application Crispin strove,
Abhorring Turk as Esquimau, the lute
As the marimba, the magnolia as rose.

Upon these premises propounding, he
Projected a colony that should extend
To the dusk of a whistling south below the south,
A comprehensive island hemisphere.
The man in Georgia waking among pines
Should be pine-spokesman. The responsive man,
Planting his pristine cores in Florida,
Should prick thereof, not on the psaltery,
But on the banjo's categorical gut,
Tuck, tuck, while the flamingos flapped his bays.
Sepulchral señors, bibbing pale mescal,
Oblivious to the Aztec almanacs,
Should make the intricate Sierra scan.
And dark Brazilians in their cafés,
Musing immaculate, pampean dits,
Should scrawl a vigilant anthology,

To be their latest, lucent paramour.
These are the broadest instances. Crispin,
Progenitor of such extensive scope,
Was not indifferent to smart detail.
The melon should have apposite ritual,
Performed in verd apparel, and the peach,
When its black branches came to bud, belle day,
Should have an incantation. And again,
When piled on salvers its aroma steeped
The summer, it should have a sacrament
And celebration. Shrewd novitiates
Should be the clerks of our experience.

These bland excursions into time to come,
Related in romance to backward flights,
However prodigal, however proud,
Contained in their afflatus the reproach
That first drove Crispin to his wandering.
He could not be content with counterfeit,
With masquerade of thought, with hapless words
That must belie the racking masquerade,
With fictive flourishes that preordained
His passion's permit, hang of coat, degree
Of buttons, measure of his salt. Such trash
Might help the blind, not him, serenely sly.
It irked beyond his patience. Hence it was,
Preferring text to gloss, he humbly served
Grotesque apprenticeship to chance event,
A clown, perhaps, but an aspiring clown.
There is a monotonous babbling in our dreams
That makes them our dependent heirs, the heirs
Of dreamers buried in our sleep, and not
The oncoming fantasies of better birth.
The apprentice knew these dreamers. If he dreamed
Their dreams, he did it in a gingerly way.
All dreams are vexing. Let them be expunged.
But let the rabbit run, the cock declaim.

Trinket pasticcio, flaunting skyey sheets,
With Crispin as the tiptoe cozener?
No, no: veracious page on page, exact.

V

A NICE SHADY HOME

Crispin as hermit, pure and capable,
Dwelt in the land. Perhaps if discontent
Had kept him still the pricking realist,
Choosing his element from droll confect
Of was and is and shall or ought to be,
Beyond Bordeaux, beyond Havana, far
Beyond carked Yucatan, he might have come
To colonize his polar planterdom
And jig his chits upon a cloudy knee.
But his emprize to that idea soon sped.
Crispin dwelt in the land and dwelling there
Slid from his continent by slow recess
To things within his actual eye, alert
To the difficulty of rebellious thought
When the sky is blue. The blue infected will.
It may be that the yarrow in his fields
Sealed pensive purple under its concern.
But day by day, now this thing and now that
Confined him, while it cosseted, condoned,
Little by little, as if the suzerain soil
Abashed him by carouse to humble yet
Attach. It seemed haphazard denouement.
He first, as realist, admitted that
Whoever hunts a matinal continent
May, after all, stop short before a plum
And be content and still be realist.
The words of things entangle and confuse.
The plum survives its poems. It may hang
In the sunshine placidly, colored by ground
Obliquities of those who pass beneath,
Harlequined and mazily dewed and mauved

In bloom. Yet it survives in its own form,
Beyond these changes, good, fat, guzzly fruit.
So Crispin hasped on the surviving form,
For him, of shall or ought to be in is.

Was he to bray this in profoundest brass
Arointing his dreams with fugal requiems?
Was he to company vastest things defunct
With a blubber of tom-toms harrowing the sky?
Scrawl a tragedian's testament? Prolong
His active force in an inactive dirge,
Which, let the tall musicians call and call,
Should merely call him dead? Pronounce amen
Through choirs infolded to the outmost clouds?
Because he built a cabin who once planned
Loquacious columns by the ructive sea?
Because he turned to salad-beds again?
Jovial Crispin, in calamitous crape?
Should he lay by the personal and make
Of his own fate an instance of all fate?
What is one man among so many men?
What are so many men in such a world?
Can one man think one thing and think it long?
Can one man be one thing and be it long?
The very man despising honest quilts
Lies quilted to his poll in his despite.
For realists, what is is what should be.

And so it came, his cabin shuffled up,
His trees were planted, his duenna brought
Her prismy blonde and clapped her in his hands,
The curtains flittered and the door was closed.
Crispin, magister of a single room,
Latched up the night. So deep a sound fell down
It was as if the solitude concealed
And covered him and his congenial sleep.
So deep a sound fell down it grew to be
A long soothsaying silence down and down.

The crickets beat their tambours in the wind,
Marching a motionless march, custodians.

In the presto of the morning, Crispin trod,
Each day, still curious, but in a round
Less prickly and much more condign than that
He once thought necessary. Like Candide,
Yeoman and grub, but with a fig in sight,
And cream for the fig and silver for the cream,
A blonde to tip the silver and to taste
The rapey gouts. Good star, how that to be
Annealed them in their cabin ribaldries!
Yet the quotidian saps philosophers
And men like Crispin like them in intent,
If not in will, to track the knaves of thought.
But the quotidian composed as his,
Of breakfast ribands, fruits laid in their leaves,
The tomtit and the cassia and the rose,
Although the rose was not the noble thorn
Of crinoline spread, but of a pining sweet,
Composed of evenings like cracked shutters flung
Upon the rumpling bottomness, and nights
In which those frail custodians watched,
Indifferent to the tepid summer cold,
While he poured out upon the lips of her
That lay beside him, the quotidian
Like this, saps like the sun, true fortuner.
For all it takes it gives a humped return
Exchequering from piebald fiscs unkeyed.

VI

AND DAUGHTERS WITH CURLS

Portentous enunciation, syllable
To blessed syllable affined, and sound
Bubbling felicity in cantilene,
Prolific and tormenting tenderness
Of music, as it comes to unison,

Forgather and bell boldly Crispin's last
Deduction. Thrum with a proud douceur
His grand pronunciamento and devise.

The chits came for his jigging, bluet-eyed,
Hands without touch yet touching poignantly,
Leaving no room upon his cloudy knee,
Prophetic joint, for its diviner young.
The return to social nature, once begun,
Anabasis or slump, ascent or chute,
Involved him in midwifery so dense
His cabin counted as phylactery,
Then place of vexing palankeens, then haunt
Of children nibbling at the sugared void,
Infants yet eminently old, then dome
And halidom for the unbraided femes,
Green crammers of the green fruits of the world,
Bidders and biders for its ecstasies,
True daughters both of Crispin and his clay.
All this with many mulctings of the man,
Effective colonizer sharply stopped
In the door-yard by his own capacious bloom.
But that this bloom grown riper, showing nibs
Of its eventual roundness, puerile tints
Of spiced and weathery rouges, should complex
The stopper to indulgent fatalist
Was unforeseen. First Crispin smiled upon
His goldenest demoiselle, inhabitant,
She seemed, of a country of the capuchins,
So delicately blushed, so humbly eyed,
Attentive to a coronal of things
Secret and singular. Second, upon
A second similar counterpart, a maid
Most sisterly to the first, not yet awake
Excepting to the motherly footstep, but
Marvelling sometimes at the shaken sleep.
Then third, a thing still flaxen in the light,
A creeper under jaunty leaves. And fourth,

Mere blusteriness that gewgaws jollified,
All din and gobble, blasphemously pink.
A few years more and the vermeil capuchin
Gave to the cabin, lordlier than it was,
The dulcet omen fit for such a house.
The second sister dallying was shy
To fetch the one full-pinioned one himself
Out of her botches, hot embosomer.
The third one gaping at the orioles
Lettered herself demurely as became
A pearly poetess, peaked for rhapsody.
The fourth, pent now, a digit curious.
Four daughters in a world too intricate
In the beginning, four blithe instruments
Of differing struts, four voices several
In couch, four more personae, intimate
As buffo, yet divers, four mirrors blue
That should be silver, four accustomed seeds
Hinting incredible hues, four self-same lights
That spread chromatics in hilarious dark,
Four questioners and four sure answerers.

Crispin concocted doctrine from the rout.
The world, a turnip once so readily plucked,
Sacked up and carried overseas, daubed out
Of its ancient purple, pruned to the fertile main,
And sown again by the stiffest realist,
Came reproduced in purple, family font,
The same insoluble lump. The fatalist
Stepped in and dropped the chuckling down his craw,
Without grace or grumble. Score this anecdote
Invented for its pith, not doctrinal
In form though in design, as Crispin willed,
Disguised pronunciamento, summary,
Autumn's compendium, strident in itself
But muted, mused, and perfectly revolved
In those portentous accents, syllables,
And sounds of music coming to accord

Upon his law, like their inherent sphere,
Seraphic proclamations of the pure
Delivered with a deluging onwardness.
Or if the music sticks, if the anecdote
Is false, if Crispin is a profitless
Philosopher, beginning with green brag,
Concluding fadedly, if as a man
Prone to distemper he abates in taste,
Fickle and fumbling, variable, obscure,
Glozing his life with after-shining flicks,
Illuminating, from a fancy gorged
By apparition, plain and common things,
Sequestering the fluster from the year,
Making gulped potions from obstreperous drops,
And so distorting, proving what he proves
Is nothing, what can all this matter since
The relation comes, benignly, to its end?

So may the relation of each man be clipped.

FROM THE MISERY OF DON JOOST

I have finished my combat with the sun;
And my body, the old animal,
Knows nothing more.

The powerful seasons bred and killed,
And were themselves the genii
Of their own ends.

Oh, but the very self of the storm
Of sun and slaves, breeding and death,
The old animal,

The senses and feeling, the very sound
And sight, and all there was of the storm,
Knows nothing more.

ANECDOTE OF MEN BY THE THOUSAND

The soul, he said, is composed
Of the external world.

There are men of the East, he said,
Who are the East.
There are men of a province
Who are that province.
There are men of a valley
Who are that valley.

There are men whose words
Are as natural sounds
Of their places
As the cackle of toucans
In the place of toucans.

The mandoline is the instrument
Of a place.

Are there mandolines of western mountains?
Are there mandolines of northern moonlight?

The dress of a woman of Lhassa,
In its place,
Is an invisible element of that place
Made visible.

FLORAL DECORATIONS FOR BANANAS

Well, nuncle, this plainly won't do.
These insolent, linear peels
And sullen, hurricane shapes
Won't do with your eglantine.
They require something serpentine.
Blunt yellow in such a room!

You should have had plums tonight,
In an eighteenth-century dish,
And pettifogging buds,
For the women of primrose and purl,
Each one in her decent curl.
Good God! What a precious light!

But bananas hacked and hunched . . .
The table was set by an ogre,
His eye on an outdoor gloom
And a stiff and noxious place.
Pile the bananas on planks.
The women will be all shanks
And bangles and slatted eyes.

And deck the bananas in leaves
Plucked from the Carib trees,
Fibrous and dangling down,
Oozing cantankerous gum
Out of their purple maws,
Darting out of their purple craws
Their musky and tingling tongues.

A HIGH-TONED OLD CHRISTIAN WOMAN

Poetry is the supreme fiction, madame.
Take the moral law and make a nave of it
And from the nave build haunted heaven. Thus,
The conscience is converted into palms,
Like windy citherns hankering for hymns.
We agree in principle. That's clear. But take
The opposing law and make a peristyle,
And from the peristyle project a masque
Beyond the planets. Thus, our bawdiness,
Unpurged by epitaph, indulged at last,
Is equally converted into palms,
Squiggling like saxophones. And palm for palm,
Madame, we are where we began. Allow,
Therefore, that in the planetary scene
Your disaffected flagellants, well-stuffed,
Smacking their muzzy bellies in parade,
Proud of such novelties of the sublime,
Such tink and tank and tunk-a-tunk-tunk,
May, merely may, madame, whip from themselves
A jovial hullabaloo among the spheres.
This will make widows wince. But fictive things
Wink as they will. Wink most when widows wince.

BANAL SOJOURN

Two wooden tubs of blue hydrangeas stand at the foot of the stone steps.
The sky is a blue gum streaked with rose. The trees are black.
The grackles crack their throats of bone in the smooth air.
Moisture and heat have swollen the garden into a slum of bloom.
Pardie! Summer is like a fat beast, sleepy in mildew,
Our old bane, green and bloated, serene, who cries,
"That bliss of stars, that princox of evening heaven!" reminding of seasons,
When radiance came running down, slim through the bareness.
And so it is one damns that green shade at the bottom of the land.
For who can care at the wigs despoiling the Satan ear?
And who does not seek the sky unfuzzed, soaring to the princox?
One has a malady, here, a malady. One feels a malady.

THE EMPEROR OF ICE-CREAM

Call the roller of big cigars,
The muscular one, and bid him whip
In kitchen cups concupiscent curds.
Let the wenches dawdle in such dress
As they are used to wear, and let the boys
Bring flowers in last month's newspapers.
Let be be finale of seem.
The only emperor is the emperor of ice-cream.

Take from the dresser of deal,
Lacking the three glass knobs, that sheet
On which she embroidered fantails once
And spread it so as to cover her face.
If her horny feet protrude, they come
To show how cold she is, and dumb.
Let the lamp affix its beam.
The only emperor is the emperor of ice-cream.

TEA AT THE PALAZ OF HOON

Not less because in purple I descended
The western day through what you called
The loneliest air, not less was I myself.

What was the ointment sprinkled on my beard?
What were the hymns that buzzed beside my ears?
What was the sea whose tide swept through me there?

Out of my mind the golden ointment rained,
And my ears made the blowing hymns they heard.
I was myself the compass of that sea:

I was the world in which I walked, and what I saw
Or heard or felt came not but from myself;
And there I found myself more truly and more strange.

DISILLUSIONMENT OF TEN O'CLOCK

The houses are haunted
By white night-gowns.
None are green,
Or purple with green rings,
Or green with yellow rings,
Or yellow with blue rings.
None of them are strange,
With socks of lace
And beaded ceintures.
People are not going
To dream of baboons and periwinkles.
Only, here and there, an old sailor,
Drunk and asleep in his boots,
Catches tigers
In red weather.

SUNDAY MORNING

I

Complacencies of the peignoir, and late
Coffee and oranges in a sunny chair,
And the green freedom of a cockatoo
Upon a rug mingle to dissipate
The holy hush of ancient sacrifice.
She dreams a little, and she feels the dark
Encroachment of that old catastrophe,
As a calm darkens among water-lights.
The pungent oranges and bright, green wings
Seem things in some procession of the dead,
Winding across wide water, without sound.
The day is like wide water, without sound,
Stilled for the passing of her dreaming feet
Over the seas, to silent Palestine,
Dominion of the blood and sepulchre.

II

Why should she give her bounty to the dead?
What is divinity if it can come
Only in silent shadows and in dreams?
Shall she not find in comforts of the sun,
In pungent fruit and bright, green wings, or else
In any balm or beauty of the earth,
Things to be cherished like the thought of heaven?
Divinity must live within herself:
Passions of rain, or moods in falling snow;
Grievings in loneliness, or unsubdued
Elations when the forest blooms; gusty
Emotions on wet roads on autumn nights;
All pleasures and all pains, remembering
The bough of summer and the winter branch.
These are the measures destined for her soul.

III

Jove in the clouds had his inhuman birth.
No mother suckled him, no sweet land gave
Large-mannered motions to his mythy mind.
He moved among us, as a muttering king,
Magnificent, would move among his hinds,
Until our blood, commingling, virginal,
With heaven, brought such requital to desire
The very hinds discerned it, in a star.
Shall our blood fail? Or shall it come to be
The blood of paradise? And shall the earth
Seem all of paradise that we shall know?
The sky will be much friendlier then than now,
A part of labor and a part of pain,
And next in glory to enduring love,
Not this dividing and indifferent blue.

IV

She says, "I am content when wakened birds,
Before they fly, test the reality
Of misty fields, by their sweet questionings;
But when the birds are gone, and their warm fields
Return no more, where, then, is paradise?"
There is not any haunt of prophecy,
Nor any old chimera of the grave,
Neither the golden underground, nor isle
Melodious, where spirits gat them home,
Nor visionary south, nor cloudy palm
Remote on heaven's hill, that has endured
As April's green endures; or will endure
Like her remembrance of awakened birds,
Or her desire for June and evening, tipped
By the consummation of the swallow's wings.

V

She says, "But in contentment I still feel
The need of some imperishable bliss."
Death is the mother of beauty; hence from her,
Alone, shall come fulfilment to our dreams
And our desires. Although she strews the leaves
Of sure obliteration on our paths,
The path sick sorrow took, the many paths
Where triumph rang its brassy phrase, or love
Whispered a little out of tenderness,
She makes the willow shiver in the sun
For maidens who were wont to sit and gaze
Upon the grass, relinquished to their feet.
She causes boys to pile new plums and pears
On disregarded plate. The maidens taste
And stray impassioned in the littering leaves.

VI

Is there no change of death in paradise?
Does ripe fruit never fall? Or do the boughs
Hang always heavy in that perfect sky,
Unchanging, yet so like our perishing earth,
With rivers like our own that seek for seas
They never find, the same receding shores
That never touch with inarticulate pang?
Why set the pear upon those river-banks
Or spice the shores with odors of the plum?
Alas, that they should wear our colors there,
The silken weavings of our afternoons,
And pick the strings of our insipid lutes!
Death is the mother of beauty, mystical,
Within whose burning bosom we devise
Our earthly mothers waiting, sleeplessly.

VII

Supple and turbulent, a ring of men
Shall chant in orgy on a summer morn
Their boisterous devotion to the sun,
Not as a god, but as a god might be,
Naked among them, like a savage source.
Their chant shall be a chant of paradise,
Out of their blood, returning to the sky;
And in their chant shall enter, voice by voice,
The windy lake wherein their lord delights,
The trees, like serafin, and echoing hills,
That choir among themselves long afterward.
They shall know well the heavenly fellowship
Of men that perish and of summer morn.
And whence they came and whither they shall go
The dew upon their feet shall manifest.

VIII

She hears, upon that water without sound,
A voice that cries, "The tomb in Palestine
Is not the porch of spirits lingering.
It is the grave of Jesus, where he lay."
We live in an old chaos of the sun,
Or old dependency of day and night,
Or island solitude, unsponsored, free,
Of that wide water, inescapable.
Deer walk upon our mountains, and the quail
Whistle about us their spontaneous cries;
Sweet berries ripen in the wilderness;
And, in the isolation of the sky,
At evening, casual flocks of pigeons make
Ambiguous undulations as they sink,
Downward to darkness, on extended wings.

SIX SIGNIFICANT LANDSCAPES

I

An old man sits
In the shadow of a pine tree
In China.
He sees larkspur,
Blue and white,
At the edge of the shadow,
Move in the wind.
His beard moves in the wind.
The pine tree moves in the wind.
Thus water flows
Over weeds.

II

The night is of the color
Of a woman's arm:
Night, the female,
Obscure,
Fragrant and supple,
Conceals herself.
A pool shines,
Like a bracelet
Shaken in a dance.

III

I measure myself
Against a tall tree.
I find that I am much taller,
For I reach right up to the sun,
With my eye;
And I reach to the shore of the sea
With my ear.
Nevertheless, I dislike
The way the ants crawl
In and out of my shadow.

IV

When my dream was near the moon,
The white folds of its gown
Filled with yellow light.
The soles of its feet
Grew red.
Its hair filled
With certain blue crystallizations
From stars,
Not far off.

V

Not all the knives of the lamp-posts,
Nor the chisels of the long streets,
Nor the mallets of the domes
And high towers,
Can carve
What one star can carve,
Shining through the grape-leaves.

VI

Rationalists, wearing square hats,
Think, in square rooms,
Looking at the floor,
Looking at the ceiling.
They confine themselves
To right-angled triangles.
If they tried rhomboids,
Cones, waving lines, ellipses—
As for example, the ellipse of the half-moon—
Rationalists would wear sombreros.

BANTAMS IN PINE-WOODS

Chieftain Iffucan of Azcan in caftan
Of tan with henna hackles, halt!

Damned universal cock, as if the sun
Was blackamoor to bear your blazing tail.

Fat! Fat! Fat! Fat! I am the personal.
Your world is you. I am my world.

You ten-foot poet among inchlings. Fat!
Begone! An inchling bristles in these pines,

Bristles, and points their Appalachian tangs,
And fears not portly Azcan nor his hoos.

ANECDOTE OF THE JAR

I placed a jar in Tennessee,
And round it was, upon a hill.
It made the slovenly wilderness
Surround that hill.

The wilderness rose up to it,
And sprawled around, no longer wild.
The jar was round upon the ground
And tall and of a port in air.

It took dominion everywhere.
The jar was gray and bare.
It did not give of bird or bush,
Like nothing else in Tennessee.

FROGS EAT BUTTERFLIES. SNAKES EAT FROGS. HOGS EAT SNAKES. MEN EAT HOGS

It is true that the rivers went nosing like swine,
Tugging at banks, until they seemed
Bland belly-sounds in somnolent troughs,

That the air was heavy with the breath of these swine,
The breath of turgid summer, and
Heavy with thunder's rattapallax,

That the man who erected this cabin, planted
This field, and tended it awhile,
Knew not the quirks of imagery,

That the hours of his indolent, arid days,
Grotesque with this nosing in banks,
This somnolence and rattapallax,

Seemed to suckle themselves on his arid being,
As the swine-like rivers suckled themselves
While they went seaward to the sea-mouths.

LIFE IS MOTION

In Oklahoma,
Bonnie and Josie,
Dressed in calico,
Danced around a stump.
They cried,
"Ohoyaho,
Ohoo" . . .
Celebrating the marriage
Of flesh and air.

GUBBINAL

That strange flower, the sun,
Is just what you say.
Have it your way.

The world is ugly,
And the people are sad.

That tuft of jungle feathers,
That animal eye,
Is just what you say.

That savage of fire,
That seed,
Have it your way.

The world is ugly,
And the people are sad.

TO THE ONE OF FICTIVE MUSIC

Sister and mother and diviner love,
And of the sisterhood of the living dead
Most near, most clear, and of the clearest bloom,
And of the fragrant mothers the most dear
And queen, and of diviner love the day
And flame and summer and sweet fire, no thread
Of cloudy silver sprinkles in your gown
Its venom of renown, and on your head
No crown is simpler than the simple hair.

Now, of the music summoned by the birth
That separates us from the wind and sea,
Yet leaves us in them, until earth becomes,
By being so much of the things we are,
Gross effigy and simulacrum, none
Gives motion to perfection more serene
Than yours, out of our imperfections wrought,
Most rare, or ever of more kindred air
In the laborious weaving that you wear.

For so retentive of themselves are men
That music is intensest which proclaims
The near, the clear, and vaunts the clearest bloom,
And of all vigils musing the obscure,
That apprehends the most which sees and names,
As in your name, an image that is sure,
Among the arrant spices of the sun,
O bough and bush and scented vine, in whom
We give ourselves our likest issuance.

Yet not too like, yet not so like to be
Too near, too clear, saving a little to endow
Our feigning with the strange unlike, whence springs
The difference that heavenly pity brings.
For this, musician, in your girdle fixed
Bear other perfumes. On your pale head wear
A band entwining, set with fatal stones.
Unreal, give back to us what once you gave:
The imagination that we spurned and crave.

PETER QUINCE AT THE CLAVIER

I

Just as my fingers on these keys
Make music, so the selfsame sounds
On my spirit make a music, too.

Music is feeling, then, not sound;
And thus it is that what I feel,
Here in this room, desiring you,

Thinking of your blue-shadowed silk,
Is music. It is like the strain
Waked in the elders by Susanna.

Of a green evening, clear and warm,
She bathed in her still garden, while
The red-eyed elders watching, felt

The basses of their beings throb
In witching chords, and their thin blood
Pulse pizzicati of Hosanna.

II

In the green water, clear and warm,
Susanna lay.
She searched
The touch of springs,
And found
Concealed imaginings.
She sighed,
For so much melody.

Upon the bank, she stood
In the cool
Of spent emotions.

She felt, among the leaves,
The dew
Of old devotions.

She walked upon the grass,
Still quavering.
The winds were like her maids,
On timid feet,
Fetching her woven scarves,
Yet wavering.

A breath upon her hand
Muted the night.
She turned—
A cymbal crashed,
And roaring horns.

III

Soon, with a noise like tambourines,
Came her attendant Byzantines.

They wondered why Susanna cried
Against the elders by her side;

And as they whispered, the refrain
Was like a willow swept by rain.

Anon, their lamps' uplifted flame
Revealed Susanna and her shame.

And then, the simpering Byzantines
Fled, with a noise like tambourines.

IV

Beauty is momentary in the mind—
The fitful tracing of a portal;
But in the flesh it is immortal.

The body dies, the body's beauty lives.
So evenings die, in their green going,
A wave, interminably flowing.
So gardens die, their meek breath scenting
The cowl of winter, done repenting.
So maidens die, to the auroral
Celebration of a maiden's choral.

Susanna's music touched the bawdy strings
Of those white elders; but, escaping,
Left only Death's ironic scraping.
Now, in its immortality, it plays
On the clear viol of her memory,
And makes a constant sacrament of praise.

THIRTEEN WAYS OF LOOKING AT A BLACKBIRD

I

Among twenty snowy mountains,
The only moving thing
Was the eye of the blackbird.

II

I was of three minds,
Like a tree
In which there are three blackbirds.

III

The blackbird whirled in the autumn winds.
It was a small part of the pantomime.

IV

A man and a woman
Are one.
A man and a woman and a blackbird
Are one.

V

I do not know which to prefer,
The beauty of inflections
Or the beauty of innuendoes,
The blackbird whistling
Or just after.

VI

Icicles filled the long window
With barbaric glass.
The shadow of the blackbird
Crossed it, to and fro.
The mood
Traced in the shadow
An indecipherable cause.

VII

O thin men of Haddam,
Why do you imagine golden birds?
Do you not see how the blackbird
Walks around the feet
Of the women about you?

VIII

I know noble accents
And lucid, inescapable rhythms;
But I know, too,
That the blackbird is involved
In what I know.

IX

When the blackbird flew out of sight,
It marked the edge
Of one of many circles.

X

At the sight of blackbirds
Flying in a green light,
Even the bawds of euphony
Would cry out sharply.

He rode over Connecticut
In a glass coach.
Once, a fear pierced him,
In that he mistook
The shadow of his equipage
For blackbirds.

XII

The river is moving.
The blackbird must be flying.

It was evening all afternoon.
It was snowing
And it was going to snow.
The blackbird sat
In the cedar-limbs.

THE MAN WHOSE PHARYNX WAS BAD

The time of year has grown indifferent.
Mildew of summer and the deepening snow
Are both alike in the routine I know.
I am too dumbly in my being pent.

The wind attendant on the solstices
Blows on the shutters of the metropoles,
Stirring no poet in his sleep, and tolls
The grand ideas of the villages.

The malady of the quotidian. . . .
Perhaps, if winter once could penetrate
Through all its purples to the final slate,
Persisting bleakly in an icy haze,

One might in turn become less diffident,
Out of such mildew plucking neater mould
And spouting new orations of the cold.
One might. One might. But time will not relent.

THE DEATH OF A SOLDIER

Life contracts and death is expected,
As in a season of autumn.
The soldier falls.

He does not become a three-days personage,
Imposing his separation,
Calling for pomp.

Death is absolute and without memorial,
As in a season of autumn,
When the wind stops,

When the wind stops and, over the heavens,
The clouds go, nevertheless,
In their direction.

SEA SURFACE FULL OF CLOUDS

I

In that November off Tehuantepec,
The slopping of the sea grew still one night
And in the morning summer hued the deck

And made one think of rosy chocolate
And gilt umbrellas. Paradisal green
Gave suavity to the perplexed machine

Of ocean, which like limpid water lay.
Who, then, in that ambrosial latitude
Out of the light evolved the moving blooms,

Who, then, evolved the sea-blooms from the clouds
Diffusing balm in that Pacific calm?
C'était mon enfant, mon bijou, mon âme.

The sea-clouds whitened far below the calm
And moved, as blooms move, in the swimming green
And in its watery radiance, while the hue

Of heaven in an antique reflection rolled
Round those flotillas. And sometimes the sea
Poured brilliant iris on the glistening blue.

II

In that November off Tehuantepec
The slopping of the sea grew still one night.
At breakfast jelly yellow streaked the deck

And made one think of chop-house chocolate
And sham umbrellas. And a sham-like green
Capped summer-seeming on the tense machine

Of ocean, which in sinister flatness lay.
Who, then, beheld the rising of the clouds
That strode submerged in that malevolent sheen,

Who saw the mortal massives of the blooms
Of water moving on the water-floor?
C'était mon frère du ciel, ma vie, mon or.

The gongs rang loudly as the windy booms
Hoo-hooed it in the darkened ocean-blooms.
The gongs grew still. And then blue heaven spread

Its crystalline pendentives on the sea
And the macabre of the water-glooms
In an enormous undulation fled.

III

In that November off Tehuantepec,
The slopping of the sea grew still one night
And a pale silver patterned on the deck

And made one think of porcelain chocolate
And pied umbrellas. An uncertain green,
Piano-polished, held the tranced machine

Of ocean, as a prelude holds and holds.
Who, seeing silver petals of white blooms
Unfolding in the water, feeling sure

Of the milk within the saltiest spurge, heard, then,
The sea unfolding in the sunken clouds?
Oh! C'était mon extase et mon amour.

So deeply sunken were they that the shrouds,
The shrouding shadows, made the petals black
Until the rolling heaven made them blue,

A blue beyond the rainy hyacinth,
And smiting the crevasses of the leaves
Deluged the ocean with a sapphire blue.

IV

In that November off Tehuantepec
The night-long slopping of the sea grew still.
A mallow morning dozed upon the deck

And made one think of musky chocolate
And frail umbrellas. A too-fluent green
Suggested malice in the dry machine

Of ocean, pondering dank stratagem.
Who then beheld the figures of the clouds
Like blooms secluded in the thick marine?

Like blooms? Like damasks that were shaken off
From the loosed girdles in the spangling must.
C'était ma foi, la nonchalance divine.

The nakedness would rise and suddenly turn
Salt masks of beard and mouths of bellowing,
Would— But more suddenly the heaven rolled

Its bluest sea-clouds in the thinking green,
And the nakedness became the broadest blooms,
Mile-mallows that a mallow sun cajoled.

V

In that November off Tehuantepec
Night stilled the slopping of the sea. The day
Came, bowing and voluble, upon the deck,

Good clown. . . . One thought of Chinese chocolate
And large umbrellas. And a motley green
Followed the drift of the obese machine

Of ocean, perfected in indolence.
What pistache one, ingenious and droll,
Beheld the sovereign clouds as jugglery

And the sea as turquoise-turbaned Sambo, neat
At tossing saucers—cloudy-conjuring sea?
C'était mon esprit bâtard, l'ignominie.

The sovereign clouds came clustering. The conch
Of loyal conjuration trumped. The wind
Of green blooms turning crisped the motley hue

To clearing opalescence. Then the sea
And heaven rolled as one and from the two
Came fresh transfigurings of freshest blue.

FAREWELL TO FLORIDA

I

Go on, high ship, since now, upon the shore,
The snake has left its skin upon the floor.
Key West sank downward under massive clouds
And silvers and greens spread over the sea. The moon
Is at the mast-head and the past is dead.
Her mind will never speak to me again.
I am free. High above the mast the moon
Rides clear of her mind and the waves make a refrain
Of this: that the snake has shed its skin upon
The floor. Go on through the darkness. The waves fly back.

II

Her mind had bound me round. The palms were hot
As if I lived in ashen ground, as if
The leaves in which the wind kept up its sound
From my North of cold whistled in a sepulchral South,
Her South of pine and coral and coraline sea,
Her home, not mine, in the ever-freshened Keys,
Her days, her oceanic nights, calling
For music, for whisperings from the reefs.
How content I shall be in the North to which I sail
And to feel sure and to forget the bleaching sand . . .

III

I hated the weathery yawl from which the pools
Disclosed the sea floor and the wilderness
Of waving weeds. I hated the vivid blooms
Curled over the shadowless hut, the rust and bones,
The trees like bones and the leaves half sand, half sun.
To stand here on the deck in the dark and say
Farewell and to know that that land is forever gone
And that she will not follow in any word
Or look, nor ever again in thought, except
That I loved her once . . . Farewell. Go on, high ship.

IV

My North is leafless and lies in a wintry slime
Both of men and clouds, a slime of men in crowds.
The men are moving as the water moves,
This darkened water cloven by sullen swells
Against your sides, then shoving and slithering,
The darkness shattered, turbulent with foam.
To be free again, to return to the violent mind
That is their mind, these men, and that will bind
Me round, carry me, misty deck, carry me
To the cold, go on, high ship, go on, plunge on.

SAILING AFTER LUNCH

It is the word *pejorative* that hurts.
My old boat goes round on a crutch
And doesn't get under way.
It's the time of the year
And the time of the day.

Perhaps it's the lunch that we had
Or the lunch that we should have had.
But I am, in any case,
A most inappropriate man
In a most unpropitious place.

Mon Dieu, hear the poet's prayer.
The romantic should be here.
The romantic should be there.
It ought to be everywhere.
But the romantic must never remain,

Mon Dieu, and must never again return.
This heavy historical sail
Through the mustiest blue of the lake
In a really vertiginous boat
Is wholly the vapidest fake. . . .

It is least what one ever sees.
It is only the way one feels, to say
Where my spirit is I am,
To say the light wind worries the sail,
To say the water is swift today,

To expunge all people and be a pupil
Of the gorgeous wheel and so to give
That slight transcendence to the dirty sail,
By light, the way one feels, sharp white,
And then rush brightly through the summer air.

SAD STRAINS OF A GAY WALTZ

The truth is that there comes a time
When we can mourn no more over music
That is so much motionless sound.

There comes a time when the waltz
Is no longer a mode of desire, a mode
Of revealing desire and is empty of shadows.

Too many waltzes have ended. And then
There's that mountain-minded Hoon,
For whom desire was never that of the waltz,

Who found all form and order in solitude,
For whom the shapes were never the figures of men.
Now, for him, his forms have vanished.

There is order in neither sea nor sun.
The shapes have lost their glistening.
There are these sudden mobs of men,

These sudden clouds of faces and arms,
An immense suppression, freed,
These voices crying without knowing for what,

Except to be happy, without knowing how,
Imposing forms they cannot describe,
Requiring order beyond their speech.

Too many waltzes have ended. Yet the shapes
For which the voices cry, these, too, may be
Modes of desire, modes of revealing desire.

Too many waltzes— The epic of disbelief
Blares oftener and soon, will soon be constant.
Some harmonious skeptic soon in a skeptical music

Will unite these figures of men and their shapes
Will glisten again with motion, the music
Will be motion and full of shadows.

HOW TO LIVE. WHAT TO DO

Last evening the moon rose above this rock
Impure upon a world unpurged.
The man and his companion stopped
To rest before the heroic height.

Coldly the wind fell upon them
In many majesties of sound:
They that had left the flame-freaked sun
To seek a sun of fuller fire.

Instead there was this tufted rock
Massively rising high and bare
Beyond all trees, the ridges thrown
Like giant arms among the clouds.

There was neither voice nor crested image,
No chorister, nor priest. There was
Only the great height of the rock
And the two of them standing still to rest.

There was the cold wind and the sound
It made, away from the muck of the land
That they had left, heroic sound
Joyous and jubilant and sure.

WAVING ADIEU, ADIEU, ADIEU

That would be waving and that would be crying,
Crying and shouting and meaning farewell,
Farewell in the eyes and farewell at the center,
Just to stand still without moving a hand.

In a world without heaven to follow, the stops
Would be endings, more poignant than partings, profounder,
And that would be saying farewell, repeating farewell,
Just to be there and just to behold.

To be one's singular self, to despise
The being that yielded so little, acquired
So little, too little to care, to turn
To the ever-jubilant weather, to sip

One's cup and never to say a word,
Or to sleep or just to lie there still,
Just to be there, just to be beheld,
That would be bidding farewell, be bidding farewell.

One likes to practice the thing. They practice,
Enough, for heaven. Ever-jubilant,
What is there here but weather, what spirit
Have I except it comes from the sun?

She sang beyond the genius of the sea.
The water never formed to mind or voice,
Like a body wholly body, fluttering
Its empty sleeves; and yet its mimic motion
Made constant cry, caused constantly a cry,
That was not ours although we understood,
Inhuman, of the veritable ocean.

The sea was not a mask. No more was she.
The song and water were not medleyed sound
Even if what she sang was what she heard,
Since what she sang was uttered word by word.
It may be that in all her phrases stirred
The grinding water and the gasping wind;
But it was she and not the sea we heard.

For she was the maker of the song she sang.
The ever-hooded, tragic-gestured sea
Was merely a place by which she walked to sing.
Whose spirit is this? we said, because we knew
It was the spirit that we sought and knew
That we should ask this often as she sang.

If it was only the dark voice of the sea
That rose, or even colored by many waves;
If it was only the outer voice of sky
And cloud, of the sunken coral water-walled,
However clear, it would have been deep air,
The heaving speech of air, a summer sound
Repeated in a summer without end
And sound alone. But it was more than that,
More even than her voice, and ours, among

The meaningless plungings of water and the wind,
Theatrical distances, bronze shadows heaped
On high horizons, mountainous atmospheres
Of sky and sea.
                        It was her voice that made
The sky acutest at its vanishing.
She measured to the hour its solitude.
She was the single artificer of the world
In which she sang. And when she sang, the sea,
Whatever self it had, became the self
That was her song, for she was the maker. Then we,
As we beheld her striding there alone,
Knew that there never was a world for her
Except the one she sang and, singing, made.

Ramon Fernandez, tell me, if you know,
Why, when the singing ended and we turned
Toward the town, tell why the glassy lights,
The lights in the fishing boats at anchor there,
As the night descended, tilting in the air,
Mastered the night and portioned out the sea,
Fixing emblazoned zones and fiery poles,
Arranging, deepening, enchanting night.

Oh! Blessed rage for order, pale Ramon,
The maker's rage to order words of the sea,
Words of the fragrant portals, dimly-starred,
And of ourselves and of our origins,
In ghostlier demarcations, keener sounds.

THE AMERICAN SUBLIME

How does one stand
To behold the sublime,
To confront the mockers,
The mickey mockers
And plated pairs?

When General Jackson
Posed for his statue
He knew how one feels.
Shall a man go barefoot
Blinking and blank?

But how does one feel?
One grows used to the weather,
The landscape and that;
And the sublime comes down
To the spirit itself,

The spirit and space,
The empty spirit
In vacant space.
What wine does one drink?
What bread does one eat?

MOZART, 1935

Poet, be seated at the piano.
Play the present, its hoo-hoo-hoo,
Its shoo-shoo-shoo, its ric-a-nic,
Its envious cachinnation.

If they throw stones upon the roof
While you practice arpeggios,
It is because they carry down the stairs
A body in rags.
Be seated at the piano.

That lucid souvenir of the past,
The divertimento;
That airy dream of the future,
The unclouded concerto . . .
The snow is falling.
Strike the piercing chord.

Be thou the voice,
Not you. Be thou, be thou
The voice of angry fear,
The voice of this besieging pain.

Be thou that wintry sound
As of the great wind howling,
By which sorrow is released,
Dismissed, absolved
In a starry placating.

We may return to Mozart.
He was young, and we, we are old.
The snow is falling
And the streets are full of cries.
Be seated, thou.

THE SUN THIS MARCH

The exceeding brightness of this early sun
Makes me conceive how dark I have become,

And re-illumines things that used to turn
To gold in broadest blue, and be a part

Of a turning spirit in an earlier self.
That, too, returns from out the winter's air,

Like an hallucination come to daze
The corner of the eye. Our element,

Cold is our element and winter's air
Brings voices as of lions coming down.

Oh! Rabbi, rabbi, fend my soul for me
And true savant of this dark nature be.

BOTANIST ON ALP (NO. I)

Panoramas are not what they used to be.
Claude has been dead a long time
And apostrophes are forbidden on the funicular.
Marx has ruined Nature,
For the moment.

For myself, I live by leaves,
So that corridors of clouds,
Corridors of cloudy thoughts,
Seem pretty much one:
I don't know what.

But in Claude how near one was
(In a world that was resting on pillars,
That was seen through arches)
To the central composition,
The essential theme.

What composition is there in all this:
Stockholm slender in a slender light,
An Adriatic *riva* rising,
Statues and stars,
Without a theme?

The pillars are prostrate, the arches are haggard,
The hotel is boarded and bare.
Yet the panorama of despair
Cannot be the specialty
Of this ecstatic air.

BOTANIST ON ALP (NO. 2)

The crosses on the convent roofs
Gleam sharply as the sun comes up.

What's down below is in the past
Like last night's crickets, far below.

And what's above is in the past
As sure as all the angels are.

Why should the future leap the clouds,
The bays of heaven, brighted, blued?

Chant, O ye faithful, in your paths
The poem of long celestial death;

For who could tolerate the earth
Without that poem, or without

An earthier one, tum, tum-ti-tum,
As of those crosses, glittering,

And merely of their glittering,
A mirror of a mere delight?

EVENING WITHOUT ANGELS

the great interests of man: air and light, the joy of
having a body, the voluptuousness of looking.
—MARIO ROSSI

Why seraphim like lutanists arranged
Above the trees? And why the poet as
Eternal *chef d'orchestre*?

                Air is air.
Its vacancy glitters round us everywhere.
Its sounds are not angelic syllables
But our unfashioned spirits realized
More sharply in more furious selves.

              And light
That fosters seraphim and is to them
Coiffeur of haloes, fecund jeweller—
Was the sun concoct for angels or for men?
Sad men made angels of the sun, and of
The moon they made their own attendant ghosts,
Which led them back to angels, after death.

Let this be clear that we are men of sun
And men of day and never of pointed night,
Men that repeat antiquest sounds of air
In an accord of repetitions. Yet,
If we repeat, it is because the wind
Encircling us, speaks always with our speech.

Light, too, encrusts us making visible
The motions of the mind and giving form
To moodiest nothings, as, desire for day
Accomplished in the immensely flashing East,
Desire for rest, in that descending sea
Of dark, which in its very darkening
Is rest and silence spreading into sleep.

. . . Evening, when the measure skips a beat
And then another, one by one, and all
To a seething minor swiftly modulate.
Bare night is best. Bare earth is best. Bare, bare,
Except for our own houses, huddled low
Beneath the arches and their spangled air,
Beneath the rhapsodies of fire and fire,
Where the voice that is in us makes a true response,
Where the voice that is great within us rises up,
As we stand gazing at the rounded moon.

RE-STATEMENT OF ROMANCE

The night knows nothing of the chants of night.
It is what it is as I am what I am:
And in perceiving this I best perceive myself

And you. Only we two may interchange
Each in the other what each has to give.
Only we two are one, not you and night,

Nor night and I, but you and I, alone,
So much alone, so deeply by ourselves,
So far beyond the casual solitudes,

That night is only the background of our selves,
Supremely true each to its separate self,
In the pale light that each upon the other throws.

THE READER

All night I sat reading a book,
Sat reading as if in a book
Of sombre pages.

It was autumn and falling stars
Covered the shrivelled forms
Crouched in the moonlight.

No lamp was burning as I read,
A voice was mumbling, "Everything
Falls back to coldness,

Even the musky muscadines,
The melons, the vermilion pears
Of the leafless garden."

The sombre pages bore no print
Except the trace of burning stars
In the frosty heaven.

ANGLAIS MORT À FLORENCE

A little less returned for him each spring.
Music began to fail him. Brahms, although
His dark familiar, often walked apart.

His spirit grew uncertain of delight,
Certain of its uncertainty, in which
That dark companion left him unconsoled

For a self returning mostly memory.
Only last year he said that the naked moon
Was not the moon he used to see, to feel

(In the pale coherences of moon and mood
When he was young), naked and alien,
More leanly shining from a lankier sky.

Its ruddy pallor had grown cadaverous.
He used his reason, exercised his will,
Turning in time to Brahms as alternate

In speech. He was that music and himself.
They were particles of order, a single majesty:
But he remembered the time when he stood alone.

He stood at last by God's help and the police;
But he remembered the time when he stood alone.
He yielded himself to that single majesty;

But he remembered the time when he stood alone,
When to be and delight to be seemed to be one,
Before the colors deepened and grew small.

THE PLEASURES OF MERELY CIRCULATING

The garden flew round with the angel,
The angel flew round with the clouds,
And the clouds flew round and the clouds flew round
And the clouds flew round with the clouds.

Is there any secret in skulls,
The cattle skulls in the woods?
Do the drummers in black hoods
Rumble anything out of their drums?

Mrs. Anderson's Swedish baby
Might well have been German or Spanish,
Yet that things go round and again go round
Has rather a classical sound.

A POSTCARD FROM THE VOLCANO

Children picking up our bones
Will never know that these were once
As quick as foxes on the hill;

And that in autumn, when the grapes
Made sharp air sharper by their smell
These had a being, breathing frost;

And least will guess that with our bones
We left much more, left what still is
The look of things, left what we felt

At what we saw. The spring clouds blow
Above the shuttered mansion-house,
Beyond our gate and the windy sky

Cries out a literate despair.
We knew for long the mansion's look
And what we said of it became

A part of what it is . . . Children,
Still weaving budded aureoles,
Will speak our speech and never know,

Will say of the mansion that it seems
As if he that lived there left behind
A spirit storming in blank walls,

A dirty house in a gutted world,
A tatter of shadows peaked to white,
Smeared with the gold of the opulent sun.

AUTUMN REFRAIN

The skreak and skritter of evening gone
And grackles gone and sorrows of the sun,
The sorrows of sun, too, gone . . . the moon and moon,
The yellow moon of words about the nightingale
In measureless measures, not a bird for me
But the name of a bird and the name of a nameless air
I have never—shall never hear. And yet beneath
The stillness of everything gone, and being still,
Being and sitting still, something resides,
Some skreaking and skrittering residuum,
And grates these evasions of the nightingale
Though I have never—shall never hear that bird.
And the stillness is in the key, all of it is,
The stillness is all in the key of that desolate sound.

GALLANT CHÂTEAU

Is it bad to have come here
And to have found the bed empty?

One might have found tragic hair,
Bitter eyes, hands hostile and cold.

There might have been a light on a book
Lighting a pitiless verse or two.

There might have been the immense solitude
Of the wind upon the curtains.

Pitiless verse? A few words tuned
And tuned and tuned and tuned.

It is good. The bed is empty,
The curtains are stiff and prim and still.

THE MAN WITH THE BLUE GUITAR

I

The man bent over his guitar,
A shearsman of sorts. The day was green.

They said, "You have a blue guitar,
You do not play things as they are."

The man replied, "Things as they are
Are changed upon the blue guitar."

And they said then, "But play, you must,
A tune beyond us, yet ourselves,

A tune upon the blue guitar
Of things exactly as they are."

II

I cannot bring a world quite round,
Although I patch it as I can.

I sing a hero's head, large eye
And bearded bronze, but not a man,

Although I patch him as I can
And reach through him almost to man.

If to serenade almost to man
Is to miss, by that, things as they are,

Say that it is the serenade
Of a man that plays a blue guitar.

III

Ah, but to play man number one,
To drive the dagger in his heart,

To lay his brain upon the board
And pick the acrid colors out,

To nail his thought across the door,
Its wings spread wide to rain and snow,

To strike his living hi and ho,
To tick it, tock it, turn it true,

To bang it from a savage blue,
Jangling the metal of the strings . . .

IV

So that's life, then: things as they are?
It picks its way on the blue guitar.

A million people on one string?
And all their manner in the thing,

And all their manner, right and wrong,
And all their manner, weak and strong?

The feelings crazily, craftily call,
Like a buzzing of flies in autumn air,

And that's life, then: things as they are,
This buzzing of the blue guitar.

V

Do not speak to us of the greatness of poetry,
Of the torches wisping in the underground,

Of the structure of vaults upon a point of light.
There are no shadows in our sun,

Day is desire and night is sleep.
There are no shadows anywhere.

The earth, for us, is flat and bare.
There are no shadows. Poetry

Exceeding music must take the place
Of empty heaven and its hymns,

Ourselves in poetry must take their place,
Even in the chattering of your guitar.

VI

A tune beyond us as we are,
Yet nothing changed by the blue guitar;

Ourselves in the tune as if in space,
Yet nothing changed, except the place

Of things as they are and only the place
As you play them, on the blue guitar,

Placed, so, beyond the compass of change,
Perceived in a final atmosphere;

For a moment final, in the way
The thinking of art seems final when

The thinking of god is smoky dew.
The tune is space. The blue guitar

Becomes the place of things as they are,
A composing of senses of the guitar.

VII

It is the sun that shares our works.
The moon shares nothing. It is a sea.

When shall I come to say of the sun,
It is a sea; it shares nothing;

The sun no longer shares our works
And the earth is alive with creeping men,

Mechanical beetles never quite warm?
And shall I then stand in the sun, as now

I stand in the moon, and call it good,
The immaculate, the merciful good,

Detached from us, from things as they are?
Not to be part of the sun? To stand

Remote and call it merciful?
The strings are cold on the blue guitar.

VIII

The vivid, florid, turgid sky,
The drenching thunder rolling by,

The morning deluged still by night,
The clouds tumultuously bright

And the feeling heavy in cold chords
Struggling toward impassioned choirs,

Crying among the clouds, enraged
By gold antagonists in air—

I know my lazy, leaden twang
Is like the reason in a storm;

And yet it brings the storm to bear.
I twang it out and leave it there.

IX

And the color, the overcast blue
Of the air, in which the blue guitar

Is a form, described but difficult,
And I am merely a shadow hunched

Above the arrowy, still strings,
The maker of a thing yet to be made;

The color like a thought that grows
Out of a mood, the tragic robe

Of the actor, half his gesture, half
His speech, the dress of his meaning, silk

Sodden with his melancholy words,
The weather of his stage, himself.

X

Raise reddest columns. Toll a bell
And clap the hollows full of tin.

Throw papers in the streets, the wills
Of the dead, majestic in their seals.

And the beautiful trombones—behold
The approach of him whom none believes,

Whom all believe that all believe,
A pagan in a varnished car.

Roll a drum upon the blue guitar.
Lean from the steeple. Cry aloud,

"Here am I, my adversary, that
Confront you, hoo-ing the slick trombones,

Yet with a petty misery
At heart, a petty misery,

Ever the prelude to your end,
The touch that topples men and rock."

XI

Slowly the ivy on the stones
Becomes the stones. Women become

The cities, children become the fields
And men in waves become the sea.

It is the chord that falsifies.
The sea returns upon the men,

The fields entrap the children, brick
Is a weed and all the flies are caught,

Wingless and withered, but living alive.
The discord merely magnifies.

Deeper within the belly's dark
Of time, time grows upon the rock.

XII

Tom-tom, c'est moi. The blue guitar
And I are one. The orchestra

Fills the high hall with shuffling men
High as the hall. The whirling noise

Of a multitude dwindles, all said,
To his breath that lies awake at night.

I know that timid breathing. Where
Do I begin and end? And where,

As I strum the thing, do I pick up
That which momentously declares

Itself not to be I and yet
Must be. It could be nothing else.

XIII

The pale intrusions into blue
Are corrupting pallors . . . ay di mi,

Blue buds or pitchy blooms. Be content—
Expansions, diffusions   content to be

The unspotted imbecile revery,
The heraldic center of the world

Of blue, blue sleek with a hundred chins,
The amorist Adjective aflame . . .

XIV

First one beam, then another, then
A thousand are radiant in the sky.

Each is both star and orb; and day
Is the riches of their atmosphere.

The sea appends its tattery hues.
The shores are banks of muffling mist.

One says a German chandelier—
A candle is enough to light the world.

It makes it clear. Even at noon
It glistens in essential dark.

At night, it lights the fruit and wine,
The book and bread, things as they are,

In a chiaroscuro where
One sits and plays the blue guitar.

XV

Is this picture of Picasso's, this "hoard
Of destructions," a picture of ourselves,

Now, an image of our society?
Do I sit, deformed, a naked egg,

Catching at Good-bye, harvest moon,
Without seeing the harvest or the moon?

Things as they are have been destroyed.
Have I? Am I a man that is dead

At a table on which the food is cold?
Is my thought a memory, not alive?

Is the spot on the floor, there, wine or blood
And whichever it may be, is it mine?

XVI

The earth is not earth but a stone,
Not the mother that held men as they fell

But stone, but like a stone, no: not
The mother, but an oppressor, but like

An oppressor that grudges them their death,
As it grudges the living that they live.

To live in war, to live at war,
To chop the sullen psaltery,

To improve the sewers in Jerusalem,
To electrify the nimbuses—

Place honey on the altars and die,
You lovers that are bitter at heart.

XVII

The person has a mould. But not
Its animal. The angelic ones

Speak of the soul, the mind. It is
An animal. The blue guitar—

On that its claws propound, its fangs
Articulate its desert days.

The blue guitar a mould? That shell?
Well, after all, the north wind blows

A horn, on which its victory
Is a worm composing on a straw.

XVIII

A dream (to call it a dream) in which
I can believe, in face of the object,

A dream no longer a dream, a thing,
Of things as they are, as the blue guitar

After long strumming on certain nights
Gives the touch of the senses, not of the hand,

But the very senses as they touch
The wind-gloss. Or as daylight comes,

Like light in a mirroring of cliffs,
Rising upward from a sea of ex.

XIX

That I may reduce the monster to
Myself, and then may be myself

In face of the monster, be more than part
Of it, more than the monstrous player of

One of its monstrous lutes, not be
Alone, but reduce the monster and be,

Two things, the two together as one,
And play of the monster and of myself,

Or better not of myself at all,
But of that as its intelligence,

Being the lion in the lute
Before the lion locked in stone.

XX

What is there in life except one's ideas,
Good air, good friend, what is there in life?

Is it ideas that I believe?
Good air, my only friend, believe,

Believe would be a brother full
Of love, believe would be a friend,

Friendlier than my only friend,
Good air. Poor pale, poor pale guitar . . .

XXI

A substitute for all the gods:
This self, not that gold self aloft,

Alone, one's shadow magnified,
Lord of the body, looking down,

As now and called most high,
The shadow of Chocorua

In an immenser heaven, aloft,
Alone, lord of the land and lord

Of the men that live in the land, high lord.
One's self and the mountains of one's land,

Without shadows, without magnificence,
The flesh, the bone, the dirt, the stone.

XXII

Poetry is the subject of the poem,
From this the poem issues and

To this returns. Between the two,
Between issue and return, there is

An absence in reality,
Things as they are. Or so we say.

But are these separate? Is it
An absence for the poem, which acquires

Its true appearances there, sun's green,
Cloud's red, earth feeling, sky that thinks?

From these it takes. Perhaps it gives,
In the universal intercourse.

XXIII

A few final solutions, like a duet
With the undertaker: a voice in the clouds,

Another on earth, the one a voice
Of ether, the other smelling of drink,

The voice of ether prevailing, the swell
Of the undertaker's song in the snow

Apostrophizing wreaths, the voice
In the clouds serene and final, next

The grunted breath serene and final,
The imagined and the real, thought

And the truth, Dichtung und Wahrheit, all
Confusion solved, as in a refrain

One keeps on playing year by year,
Concerning the nature of things as they are.

XXIV

A poem like a missal found
In the mud, a missal for that young man,

That scholar hungriest for that book,
The very book, or, less, a page

Or, at the least, a phrase, that phrase,
A hawk of life, that latined phrase:

To know; a missal for brooding-sight.
To meet that hawk's eye and to flinch

Not at the eye but at the joy of it.
I play. But this is what I think.

XXV

He held the world upon his nose
And this-a-way he gave a fling.

His robes and symbols, ai-yi-yi—
And that-a-way he twirled the thing.

Sombre as fir-trees, liquid cats
Moved in the grass without a sound.

They did not know the grass went round.
The cats had cats and the grass turned gray

And the world had worlds, ai, this-a-way:
The grass turned green and the grass turned gray.

And the nose is eternal, that-a-way.
Things as they were, things as they are,

Things as they will be by and by . . .
A fat thumb beats out ai-yi-yi.

XXVI

The world washed in his imagination,
The world was a shore, whether sound or form

Or light, the relic of farewells,
Rock, of valedictory echoings,

To which his imagination returned,
From which it sped, a bar in space,

Sand heaped in the clouds, giant that fought
Against the murderous alphabet:

The swarm of thoughts, the swarm of dreams
Of inaccessible Utopia.

A mountainous music always seemed
To be falling and to be passing away.

XXVII

It is the sea that whitens the roof.
The sea drifts through the winter air.

It is the sea that the north wind makes.
The sea is in the falling snow.

This gloom is the darkness of the sea.
Geographers and philosophers,

Regard. But for that salty cup,
But for the icicles on the eaves—

The sea is a form of ridicule.
The iceberg settings satirize

The demon that cannot be himself,
That tours to shift the shifting scene.

XXVIII

I am a native in this world
And think in it as a native thinks,

Gesu, not native of a mind
Thinking the thoughts I call my own,

Native, a native in the world
And like a native think in it.

It could not be a mind, the wave
In which the watery grasses flow

And yet are fixed as a photograph,
The wind in which the dead leaves blow.

Here I inhale profounder strength
And as I am, I speak and move

And things are as I think they are
And say they are on the blue guitar.

XXIX

In the cathedral, I sat there, and read,
Alone, a lean Review and said,

"These degustations in the vaults
Oppose the past and the festival.

What is beyond the cathedral, outside,
Balances with nuptial song.

So it is to sit and to balance things
To and to and to the point of still,

To say of one mask it is like,
To say of another it is like,

To know that the balance does not quite rest,
That the mask is strange, however like."

The shapes are wrong and the sounds are false.
The bells are the bellowings of bulls.

Yet Franciscan don was never more
Himself than in this fertile glass.

XXX

From this I shall evolve a man.
This is his essence: the old fantoche

Hanging his shawl upon the wind,
Like something on the stage, puffed out,

His strutting studied through centuries.
At last, in spite of his manner, his eye

A-cock at the cross-piece on a pole
Supporting heavy cables, slung

Through Oxidia, banal suburb,
One-half of all its installments paid.

Dew-dapper clapper-traps, blazing
From crusty stacks above machines.

Ecce, Oxidia is the seed
Dropped out of this amber-ember pod,

Oxidia is the soot of fire,
Oxidia is Olympia.

XXXI

How long and late the pheasant sleeps . . .
The employer and employee contend,

Combat, compose their droll affair.
The bubbling sun will bubble up,

Spring sparkle and the cock-bird shriek.
The employer and employee will hear

And continue their affair. The shriek
Will rack the thickets. There is no place,

Here, for the lark fixed in the mind,
In the museum of the sky. The cock

Will claw sleep. Morning is not sun,
It is this posture of the nerves,

As if a blunted player clutched
The nuances of the blue guitar.

It must be this rhapsody or none,
The rhapsody of things as they are.

XXXII

Throw away the lights, the definitions,
And say of what you see in the dark

That it is this or that it is that,
But do not use the rotted names.

How should you walk in that space and know
Nothing of the madness of space,

Nothing of its jocular procreations?
Throw the lights away. Nothing must stand

Between you and the shapes you take
When the crust of shape has been destroyed.

You as you are? You are yourself.
The blue guitar surprises you.

XXXIII

That generation's dream, aviled
In the mud, in Monday's dirty light,

That's it, the only dream they knew,
Time in its final block, not time

To come, a wrangling of two dreams.
Here is the bread of time to come,

Here is its actual stone. The bread
Will be our bread, the stone will be

Our bed and we shall sleep by night.
We shall forget by day, except

The moments when we choose to play
The imagined pine, the imagined jay.

THE MEN THAT ARE FALLING

God and all angels sing the world to sleep,
Now that the moon is rising in the heat

And crickets are loud again in the grass. The moon
Burns in the mind on lost remembrances.

He lies down and the night wind blows upon him here.
The bells grow longer. This is not sleep. This is desire.

Ah! Yes, desire . . . this leaning on his bed,
This leaning on his elbows on his bed,

Staring, at midnight, at the pillow that is black
In the catastrophic room . . . beyond despair,

Like an intenser instinct. What is it he desires?
But this he cannot know, the man that thinks,

Yet life itself, the fulfilment of desire
In the grinding ric-rac, staring steadily

At a head upon the pillow in the dark,
More than sudarium, speaking the speech

Of absolutes, bodiless, a head
Thick-lipped from riot and rebellious cries,

The head of one of the men that are falling, placed
Upon the pillow to repose and speak,

Speak and say the immaculate syllables
That he spoke only by doing what he did.

God and all angels, this was his desire,
Whose head lies blurring here, for this he died.

Taste of the blood upon his martyred lips,
O pensioners, O demagogues and pay-men!

This death was his belief though death is a stone.
This man loved earth, not heaven, enough to die.

The night wind blows upon the dreamer, bent
Over words that are life's voluble utterance.

POETRY IS A DESTRUCTIVE FORCE

That's what misery is,
Nothing to have at heart.
It is to have or nothing.

It is a thing to have,
A lion, an ox in his breast,
To feel it breathing there.

Corazon, stout dog,
Young ox, bow-legged bear,
He tastes its blood, not spit.

He is like a man
In the body of a violent beast.
Its muscles are his own . . .

The lion sleeps in the sun.
Its nose is on its paws.
It can kill a man.

THE POEMS OF OUR CLIMATE

I

Clear water in a brilliant bowl,
Pink and white carnations. The light
In the room more like a snowy air,
Reflecting snow. A newly-fallen snow
At the end of winter when afternoons return.
Pink and white carnations—one desires
So much more than that. The day itself
Is simplified: a bowl of white,
Cold, a cold porcelain, low and round,
With nothing more than the carnations there.

II

Say even that this complete simplicity
Stripped one of all one's torments, concealed
The evilly compounded, vital I
And made it fresh in a world of white,
A world of clear water, brilliant-edged,
Still one would want more, one would need more,
More than a world of white and snowy scents.

III

There would still remain the never-resting mind,
So that one would want to escape, come back
To what had been so long composed.
The imperfect is our paradise.
Note that, in this bitterness, delight,
Since the imperfect is so hot in us,
Lies in flawed words and stubborn sounds.

STUDY OF TWO PEARS

I

Opusculum paedagogum.
The pears are not viols,
Nudes or bottles.
They resemble nothing else.

II

They are yellow forms
Composed of curves
Bulging toward the base.
They are touched red.

III

They are not flat surfaces
Having curved outlines.
They are round
Tapering toward the top.

IV

In the way they are modelled
There are bits of blue.
A hard dry leaf hangs
From the stem.

V

The yellow glistens.
It glistens with various yellows,
Citrons, oranges and greens
Flowering over the skin.

VI

The shadows of the pears
Are blobs on the green cloth.
The pears are not seen
As the observer wills.

THE GLASS OF WATER

That the glass would melt in heat,
That the water would freeze in cold,
Shows that this object is merely a state,
One of many, between two poles. So,
In the metaphysical, there are these poles.

Here in the center stands the glass. Light
Is the lion that comes down to drink. There
And in that state, the glass is a pool.
Ruddy are his eyes and ruddy are his claws
When light comes down to wet his frothy jaws

And in the water winding weeds move round.
And there and in another state—the refractions,
The *metaphysica*, the plastic parts of poems
Crash in the mind— But, fat Jocundus, worrying
About what stands here in the center, not the glass,

But in the center of our lives, this time, this day,
It is a state, this spring among the politicians
Playing cards. In a village of the indigenes,
One would have still to discover. Among the dogs and dung,
One would continue to contend with one's ideas.

ADD THIS TO RHETORIC

It is posed and it is posed.
But in nature it merely grows.
Stones pose in the falling night;
And beggars dropping to sleep,
They pose themselves and their rags.
Shucks . . . lavender moonlight falls.
The buildings pose in the sky
And, as you paint, the clouds,
Grisaille, impearled, profound,
Pftt . . . In the way you speak
You arrange, the thing is posed,
What in nature merely grows.

To-morrow when the sun,
For all your images,
Comes up as the sun, bull fire,
Your images will have left
No shadow of themselves.
The poses of speech, of paint,
Of music— Her body lies
Worn out, her arm falls down,
Her fingers touch the ground.
Above her, to the left,
A brush of white, the obscure,
The moon without a shape,
A fringed eye in a crypt.
The sense creates the pose.
In this it moves and speaks.
This is the figure and not
An evading metaphor.

Add this. It is to add.

THE MAN ON THE DUMP

Day creeps down. The moon is creeping up.
The sun is a corbeil of flowers the moon Blanche
Places there, a bouquet. Ho-ho . . . The dump is full
Of images. Days pass like papers from a press.
The bouquets come here in the papers. So the sun,
And so the moon, both come, and the janitor's poems
Of every day, the wrapper on the can of pears,
The cat in the paper-bag, the corset, the box
From Esthonia: the tiger chest, for tea.

The freshness of night has been fresh a long time.
The freshness of morning, the blowing of day, one says
That it puffs as Cornelius Nepos reads, it puffs
More than, less than or it puffs like this or that.
The green smacks in the eye, the dew in the green
Smacks like fresh water in a can, like the sea
On a cocoanut—how many men have copied dew
For buttons, how many women have covered themselves
With dew, dew dresses, stones and chains of dew, heads
Of the floweriest flowers dewed with the dewiest dew.
One grows to hate these things except on the dump.

Now, in the time of spring (azaleas, trilliums,
Myrtle, viburnums, daffodils, blue phlox),
Between that disgust and this, between the things
That are on the dump (azaleas and so on)
And those that will be (azaleas and so on),
One feels the purifying change. One rejects
The trash.
            That's the moment when the moon creeps up
To the bubbling of bassoons. That's the time
One looks at the elephant-colorings of tires.
Everything is shed; and the moon comes up as the moon
(All its images are in the dump) and you see
As a man (not like an image of a man),
You see the moon rise in the empty sky.

One sits and beats an old tin can, lard pail.
One beats and beats for that which one believes.
That's what one wants to get near. Could it after all
Be merely oneself, as superior as the ear
To a crow's voice? Did the nightingale torture the ear,
Pack the heart and scratch the mind? And does the ear
Solace itself in peevish birds? Is it peace,
Is it a philosopher's honeymoon, one finds
On the dump? Is it to sit among mattresses of the dead,
Bottles, pots, shoes and grass and murmur *aptest eve:*
Is it to hear the blatter of grackles and say
Invisible priest; is it to eject, to pull
The day to pieces and cry *stanza my stone?*
Where was it one first heard of the truth? The the.

ON THE ROAD HOME

It was when I said,
"There is no such thing as the truth,"
That the grapes seemed fatter.
The fox ran out of his hole.

You . . . You said,
"There are many truths,
But they are not parts of a truth."
Then the tree, at night, began to change,

Smoking through green and smoking blue.
We were two figures in a wood.
We said we stood alone.

It was when I said,
"Words are not forms of a single word.
In the sum of the parts, there are only the parts.
The world must be measured by eye";

It was when you said,
"The idols have seen lots of poverty,
Snakes and gold and lice,
But not the truth";

It was at that time, that the silence was largest
And longest, the night was roundest,
The fragrance of the autumn warmest,
Closest and strongest.

THE LATEST FREED MAN

Tired of the old descriptions of the world,
The latest freed man rose at six and sat
On the edge of his bed. He said,
                              "I suppose there is
A doctrine to this landscape. Yet, having just
Escaped from the truth, the morning is color and mist,
Which is enough: the moment's rain and sea,
The moment's sun (the strong man vaguely seen),
Overtaking the doctrine of this landscape. Of him
And of his works, I am sure. He bathes in the mist
Like a man without a doctrine. The light he gives—
It is how he gives his light. It is how he shines,
Rising upon the doctors in their beds
And on their beds. . . ."
                              And so the freed man said.
It was how the sun came shining into his room:
To be without a description of to be,
For a moment on rising, at the edge of the bed, to be,
To have the ant of the self changed to an ox
With its organic boomings, to be changed
From a doctor into an ox, before standing up,
To know that the change and that the ox-like struggle
Come from the strength that is the strength of the sun,
Whether it comes directly or from the sun.
It was how he was free. It was how his freedom came.
It was being without description, being an ox.
It was the importance of the trees outdoors,
The freshness of the oak-leaves, not so much
That they were oak-leaves, as the way they looked.
It was everything being more real, himself
At the center of reality, seeing it.
It was everything bulging and blazing and big in itself,
The blue of the rug, the portrait of Vidal,
Qui fait fi des joliesses banales, the chairs.

THE DWARF

Now it is September and the web is woven.
The web is woven and you have to wear it.

The winter is made and you have to bear it,
The winter web, the winter woven, wind and wind,

For all the thoughts of summer that go with it
In the mind, pupa of straw, moppet of rags.

It is the mind that is woven, the mind that was jerked
And tufted in straggling thunder and shattered sun.

It is all that you are, the final dwarf of you,
That is woven and woven and waiting to be worn,

Neither as mask nor as garment but as a being,
Torn from insipid summer, for the mirror of cold,

Sitting beside your lamp, there citron to nibble
And coffee dribble . . . Frost is in the stubble.

A RABBIT AS KING OF THE GHOSTS

The difficulty to think at the end of day,
When the shapeless shadow covers the sun
And nothing is left except light on your fur—

There was the cat slopping its milk all day,
Fat cat, red tongue, green mind, white milk
And August the most peaceful month.

To be, in the grass, in the peacefullest time,
Without that monument of cat,
The cat forgotten in the moon;

And to feel that the light is a rabbit-light,
In which everything is meant for you
And nothing need be explained;

Then there is nothing to think of. It comes of itself;
And east rushes west and west rushes down,
No matter. The grass is full

And full of yourself. The trees around are for you,
The whole of the wideness of night is for you,
A self that touches all edges,

You become a self that fills the four corners of night.
The red cat hides away in the fur-light
And there you are humped high, humped up,

You are humped higher and higher, black as stone—
You sit with your head like a carving in space
And the little green cat is a bug in the grass.

GIRL IN A NIGHTGOWN

Lights out. Shades up.
A look at the weather.
There has been a booming all the spring,
A refrain from the end of the boulevards.

This is the silence of night,
This is what could not be shaken,
Full of stars and the images of stars—
And that booming wintry and dull,

Like a tottering, a falling and an end,
Again and again, always there,
Massive drums and leaden trumpets,
Perceived by feeling instead of sense,

A revolution of things colliding.
Phrases! But of fear and of fate.
The night should be warm and fluters' fortune
Should play in the trees when morning comes.

Once it was, the repose of night,
Was a place, strong place, in which to sleep.
It is shaken now. It will burst into flames,
Either now or tomorrow or the day after that.

CONNOISSEUR OF CHAOS

I

A. A violent order is disorder; and
B. A great disorder is an order. These
Two things are one. (Pages of illustrations.)

II

If all the green of spring was blue, and it is;
If the flowers of South Africa were bright
On the tables of Connecticut, and they are;
If Englishmen lived without tea in Ceylon, and they do;
And if it all went on in an orderly way,
And it does; a law of inherent opposites,
Of essential unity, is as pleasant as port,
As pleasant as the brush-strokes of a bough,
An upper, particular bough in, say, Marchand.

III

After all the pretty contrast of life and death
Proves that these opposite things partake of one,
At least that was the theory, when bishops' books
Resolved the world. We cannot go back to that.
The squirming facts exceed the squamous mind,
If one may say so. And yet relation appears,
A small relation expanding like the shade
Of a cloud on sand, a shape on the side of a hill.

IV

A. Well, an old order is a violent one.
This proves nothing. Just one more truth, one more
Element in the immense disorder of truths.
B. It is April as I write. The wind
Is blowing after days of constant rain.
All this, of course, will come to summer soon.
But suppose the disorder of truths should ever come
To an order, most Plantagenet, most fixed . . .
A great disorder is an order. Now, A
And B are not like statuary, posed
For a vista in the Louvre. They are things chalked
On the sidewalk so that the pensive man may see.

V

The pensive man . . . He sees that eagle float
For which the intricate Alps are a single nest.

A sunny day's complete Poussiniana
Divide it from itself. It is this or that
And it is not.
               By metaphor you paint
A thing. Thus, the pineapple was a leather fruit,
A fruit for pewter, thorned and palmed and blue,
To be served by men of ice.
                              The senses paint
By metaphor. The juice was fragranter
Than wettest cinnamon. It was cribled pears
Dripping a morning sap.
                        The truth must be
That you do not see, you experience, you feel,
That the buxom eye brings merely its element
To the total thing, a shapeless giant forced
Upward.
          Green were the curls upon that head.

THE COMMON LIFE

That's the down-town frieze,
Principally the church steeple,
A black line beside a white line;
And the stack of the electric plant,
A black line drawn on flat air.

It is a morbid light
In which they stand,
Like an electric lamp
On a page of Euclid.

In this light a man is a result,
A demonstration, and a woman,
Without rose and without violet,
The shadows that are absent from Euclid,
Is not a woman for a man.

The paper is whiter
For these black lines.
It glares beneath the webs
Of wire, the designs of ink,
The planes that ought to have genius,
The volumes like marble ruins
Outlined and having alphabetical
Notations and footnotes.
The paper is whiter.
The men have no shadows
And the women have only one side.

THE SENSE OF THE SLEIGHT-OF-HAND MAN

One's grand flights, one's Sunday baths,
One's tootings at the weddings of the soul
Occur as they occur. So bluish clouds
Occurred above the empty house and the leaves
Of the rhododendrons rattled their gold,
As if someone lived there. Such floods of white
Came bursting from the clouds. So the wind
Threw its contorted strength around the sky.

Could you have said the bluejay suddenly
Would swoop to earth? It is a wheel, the rays
Around the sun. The wheel survives the myths.
The fire eye in the clouds survives the gods.
To think of a dove with an eye of grenadine
And pines that are cornets, so it occurs,
And a little island full of geese and stars:
It may be that the ignorant man, alone,
Has any chance to mate his life with life
That is the sensual, pearly spouse, the life
That is fluent in even the wintriest bronze.

A DISH OF PEACHES IN RUSSIA

With my whole body I taste these peaches,
I touch them and smell them. Who speaks?

I absorb them as the Angevine
Absorbs Anjou. I see them as a lover sees,

As a young lover sees the first buds of spring
And as the black Spaniard plays his guitar.

Who speaks? But it must be that I,
That animal, that Russian, that exile, for whom

The bells of the chapel pullulate sounds at
Heart. The peaches are large and round,

Ah! and red; and they have peach fuzz, ah!
They are full of juice and the skin is soft.

They are full of the colors of my village
And of fair weather, summer, dew, peace.

The room is quiet where they are.
The windows are open. The sunlight fills

The curtains. Even the drifting of the curtains,
Slight as it is, disturbs me. I did not know

That such ferocities could tear
One self from another, as these peaches do.

OF HARTFORD IN A PURPLE LIGHT

A long time you have been making the trip
From Havre to Hartford, Master Soleil,
Bringing the lights of Norway and all that.

A long time the ocean has come with you,
Shaking the water off, like a poodle,
That splatters incessant thousands of drops,

Each drop a petty tricolor. For this,
The aunts in Pasadena, remembering,
Abhor the plaster of the western horses,

Souvenirs of museums. But, Master, there are
Lights masculine and lights feminine.
What is this purple, this parasol,

This stage-light of the Opera?
It is like a region full of intonings.
It is Hartford seen in a purple light.

A moment ago, light masculine,
Working, with big hands, on the town,
Arranged its heroic attitudes.

But now as in an amour of women
Purple sets purple round. Look, Master,
See the river, the railroad, the cathedral . . .

When male light fell on the naked back
Of the town, the river, the railroad were clear.
Now, every muscle slops away.

Hi! Whisk it, poodle, flick the spray
Of the ocean, ever-freshening,
On the irised hunks, the stone bouquet.

BOUQUET OF BELLE SCAVOIR

I

It is she alone that matters.
She made it. It is easy to say
The figures of speech, as why she chose
This dark, particular rose.

II

Everything in it is herself.
Yet the freshness of the leaves, the burn
Of the colors, are tinsel changes,
Out of the changes of both light and dew.

III

How often had he walked
Beneath summer and the sky
To receive her shadow into his mind . . .
Miserable that it was not she.

IV

The sky is too blue, the earth too wide.
The thought of her takes her away.
The form of her in something else
Is not enough.

V

The reflection of her here, and then there,
Is another shadow, another evasion,
Another denial. If she is everywhere,
She is nowhere, to him.

VI

But this she has made. If it is
Another image, it is one she has made.
It is she that he wants, to look at directly,
Someone before him to see and to know.

YELLOW AFTERNOON

It was in the earth only
That he was at the bottom of things
And of himself. There he could say
Of this I am, this is the patriarch,
This it is that answers when I ask,
This is the mute, the final sculpture
Around which silence lies on silence.
This reposes alike in springtime
And, arbored and bronzed, in autumn.

He said I had this that I could love,
As one loves visible and responsive peace,
As one loves one's own being,
As one loves that which is the end
And must be loved, as one loves that
Of which one is a part as in a unity,
A unity that is the life one loves,
So that one lives all the lives that comprise it
As the life of the fatal unity of war.

Everything comes to him
From the middle of his field. The odor
Of earth penetrates more deeply than any word.
There he touches his being. There as he is
He is. The thought that he had found all this
Among men, in a woman—she caught his breath—
But he came back as one comes back from the sun
To lie on one's bed in the dark, close to a face
Without eyes or mouth, that looks at one and speaks.

MARTIAL CADENZA

I

Only this evening I saw again low in the sky
The evening star, at the beginning of winter, the star
That in spring will crown every western horizon,
Again . . . as if it came back, as if life came back,
Not in a later son, a different daughter, another place,
But as if evening found us young, still young,
Still walking in a present of our own.

II

It was like sudden time in a world without time,
This world, this place, the street in which I was,
Without time: as that which is not has no time,
Is not, or is of what there was, is full
Of the silence before the armies, armies without
Either trumpets or drums, the commanders mute, the arms
On the ground, fixed fast in a profound defeat.

III

What had this star to do with the world it lit,
With the blank skies over England, over France
And above the German camps? It looked apart.
Yet it is this that shall maintain— Itself
Is time, apart from any past, apart
From any future, the ever-living and being,
The ever-breathing and moving, the constant fire,

IV

The present close, the present realized,
Not the symbol but that for which the symbol stands,
The vivid thing in the air that never changes,
Though the air change. Only this evening I saw it again,
At the beginning of winter, and I walked and talked
Again, and lived and was again, and breathed again
And moved again and flashed again, time flashed again.

The poem of the mind in the act of finding
What will suffice. It has not always had
To find: the scene was set; it repeated what
Was in the script.
                              Then the theatre was changed
To something else. Its past was a souvenir.

It has to be living, to learn the speech of the place.
It has to face the men of the time and to meet
The women of the time. It has to think about war
And it has to find what will suffice. It has
To construct a new stage. It has to be on that stage
And, like an insatiable actor, slowly and
With meditation, speak words that in the ear,
In the delicatest ear of the mind, repeat,
Exactly, that which it wants to hear, at the sound
Of which, an invisible audience listens,
Not to the play, but to itself, expressed
In an emotion as of two people, as of two
Emotions becoming one. The actor is
A metaphysician in the dark, twanging
An instrument, twanging a wiry string that gives
Sounds passing through sudden rightnesses, wholly
Containing the mind, below which it cannot descend,
Beyond which it has no will to rise.
                              It must
Be the finding of a satisfaction, and may
Be of a man skating, a woman dancing, a woman
Combing. The poem of the act of the mind.

ARRIVAL AT THE WALDORF

Home from Guatemala, back at the Waldorf.
This arrival in the wild country of the soul,
All approaches gone, being completely there,

Where the wild poem is a substitute
For the woman one loves or ought to love,
One wild rhapsody a fake for another.

You touch the hotel the way you touch moonlight
Or sunlight and you hum and the orchestra
Hums and you say "The world in a verse,

A generation sealed, men remoter than mountains,
Women invisible in music and motion and color,"
After that alien, point-blank, green and actual Guatemala.

LANDSCAPE WITH BOAT

An anti-master-man, floribund ascetic.

He brushed away the thunder, then the clouds,
Then the colossal illusion of heaven. Yet still
The sky was blue. He wanted imperceptible air.
He wanted to see. He wanted the eye to see
And not be touched by blue. He wanted to know,
A naked man who regarded himself in the glass
Of air, who looked for the world beneath the blue,
Without blue, without any turquoise tint or phase,
Any azure under-side or after-color. Nabob
Of bones, he rejected, he denied, to arrive
At the neutral center, the ominous element,
The single-colored, colorless, primitive.

It was not as if the truth lay where he thought,
Like a phantom, in an uncreated night.
It was easier to think it lay there. If
It was nowhere else, it was there and because
It was nowhere else, its place had to be supposed,
Itself had to be supposed, a thing supposed
In a place supposed, a thing that he reached
In a place that he reached, by rejecting what he saw
And denying what he heard. He would arrive.
He had only not to live, to walk in the dark,
To be projected by one void into
Another.
       It was his nature to suppose,
To receive what others had supposed, without
Accepting. He received what he denied.
But as truth to be accepted, he supposed
A truth beyond all truths.
              He never supposed
That he might be truth, himself, or part of it,
That the things that he rejected might be part
And the irregular turquoise, part, the perceptible blue
Grown denser, part, the eye so touched, so played
Upon by clouds, the ear so magnified

By thunder, parts, and all these things together,
Parts, and more things, parts. He never supposed divine
Things might not look divine, nor that if nothing
Was divine then all things were, the world itself,
And that if nothing was the truth, then all
Things were the truth, the world itself was the truth.

Had he been better able to suppose:
He might sit on a sofa on a balcony
Above the Mediterranean, emerald
Becoming emeralds. He might watch the palms
Flap green ears in the heat. He might observe
A yellow wine and follow a steamer's track
And say, "The thing I hum appears to be
The rhythm of this celestial pantomime."

ON THE ADEQUACY OF LANDSCAPE

The little owl flew through the night,
As if the people in the air
Were frightened and he frightened them,
By being there,

The people that turned off and came
To avoid the bright, discursive wings,
To avoid the hap-hallow hallow-ho
Of central things,

Nor in their empty hearts to feel
The blood-red redness of the sun,
To shrink to an insensible,
Small oblivion,

Beyond the keenest diamond day
Of people sensible to pain,
When cocks wake, clawing at their beds
To be again,

And who, for that, turn toward the cocks
And toward the start of day and trees
And light behind the body of night
And sun, as if these

Were what they are, the sharpest sun:
The sharpest self, the sensible range,
The extent of what they are, the strength
That they exchange,

So that he that suffers most desires
The red bird most and the strongest sky—
Not the people in the air that hear
The little owl fly.

WOMAN LOOKING AT A VASE OF FLOWERS

It was as if thunder took form upon
The piano, that time: the time when the crude
And jealous grandeurs of sun and sky
Scattered themselves in the garden, like
The wind dissolving into birds,
The clouds becoming braided girls.
It was like the sea poured out again
In east wind beating the shutters at night.

Hoot, little owl within her, how
High blue became particular
In the leaf and bud and how the red,
Flicked into pieces, points of air,
Became—how the central, essential red
Escaped its large abstraction, became,
First, summer, then a lesser time,
Then the sides of peaches, of dusky pears.

Hoot how the inhuman colors fell
Into place beside her, where she was,
Like human conciliations, more like
A profounder reconciling, an act,
An affirmation free from doubt.
The crude and jealous formlessness
Became the form and the fragrance of things
Without clairvoyance, close to her.

THE WELL DRESSED MAN WITH A BEARD

After the final no there comes a yes
And on that yes the future world depends.
No was the night. Yes is this present sun.
If the rejected things, the things denied,
Slid over the western cataract, yet one,
One only, one thing that was firm, even
No greater than a cricket's horn, no more
Than a thought to be rehearsed all day, a speech
Of the self that must sustain itself on speech,
One thing remaining, infallible, would be
Enough. Ah! douce campagna of that thing!
Ah! douce campagna, honey in the heart,
Green in the body, out of a petty phrase,
Out of a thing believed, a thing affirmed:
The form on the pillow humming while one sleeps,
The aureole above the humming house . . .

It can never be satisfied, the mind, never.

OF BRIGHT & BLUE BIRDS & THE GALA SUN

Some things, niño, some things are like this,
That instantly and in themselves they are gay
And you and I are such things, O most miserable . . .

For a moment they are gay and are a part
Of an element, the exactest element for us,
In which we pronounce joy like a word of our own.

It is there, being imperfect, and with these things
And erudite in happiness, with nothing learned,
That we are joyously ourselves and we think

Without the labor of thought, in that element,
And we feel, in a way apart, for a moment, as if
There was a bright *scienza* outside of ourselves,

A gaiety that is being, not merely knowing,
The will to be and to be total in belief,
Provoking a laughter, an agreement, by surprise.

MRS. ALFRED URUGUAY

So what said the others and the sun went down
And, in the brown blues of evening, the lady said,
In the donkey's ear, "I fear that elegance
Must struggle like the rest." She climbed until
The moonlight in her lap, mewing her velvet,
And her dress were one and she said, "I have said no
To everything, in order to get at myself.
I have wiped away moonlight like mud. Your innocent ear
And I, if I rode naked, are what remain."

The moonlight crumbled to degenerate forms,
While she approached the real, upon her mountain,
With lofty darkness. The donkey was there to ride,
To hold by the ear, even though it wished for a bell,
Wished faithfully for a falsifying bell.
Neither the moonlight could change it. And for her,
To be, regardless of velvet, could never be more
Than to be, she could never differently be,
Her no and no made yes impossible.

Who was it passed her there on a horse all will,
What figure of capable imagination?
Whose horse clattered on the road on which she rose,
As it descended, blind to her velvet and
The moonlight? Was it a rider intent on the sun,
A youth, a lover with phosphorescent hair,
Dressed poorly, arrogant of his streaming forces,
Lost in an integration of the martyrs' bones,
Rushing from what was real; and capable?

The villages slept as the capable man went down,
Time swished on the village clocks and dreams were alive,
The enormous gongs gave edges to their sounds,
As the rider, no chevalere and poorly dressed,
Impatient of the bells and midnight forms,
Rode over the picket rocks, rode down the road,
And, capable, created in his mind,
Eventual victor, out of the martyrs' bones,
The ultimate elegance: the imagined land.

ASIDES ON THE OBOE

The prologues are over. It is a question, now,
Of final belief. So, say that final belief
Must be in a fiction. It is time to choose.

I

That obsolete fiction of the wide river in
An empty land; the gods that Boucher killed;
And the metal heroes that time granulates—
The philosophers' man alone still walks in dew,
Still by the sea-side mutters milky lines
Concerning an immaculate imagery.
If you say on the hautboy man is not enough,
Can never stand as god, is ever wrong
In the end, however naked, tall, there is still
The impossible possible philosophers' man,
The man who has had the time to think enough,
The central man, the human globe, responsive
As a mirror with a voice, the man of glass,
Who in a million diamonds sums us up.

II

He is the transparence of the place in which
He is and in his poems we find peace.
He sets this peddler's pie and cries in summer,
The glass man, cold and numbered, dewily cries,
"Thou art not August unless I make thee so."
Clandestine steps upon imagined stairs
Climb through the night, because his cuckoos call.

III

One year, death and war prevented the jasmine scent
And the jasmine islands were bloody martyrdoms.
How was it then with the central man? Did we
Find peace? We found the sum of men. We found,
If we found the central evil, the central good.
We buried the fallen without jasmine crowns.
There was nothing he did not suffer, no; nor we.

It was not as if the jasmine ever returned.
But we and the diamond globe at last were one.
We had always been partly one. It was as we came
To see him, that we were wholly one, as we heard
Him chanting for those buried in their blood,
In the jasmine haunted forests, that we knew
The glass man, without external reference.

METAMORPHOSIS

Yillow, yillow, yillow,
Old worm, my pretty quirk,
How the wind spells out
Sep - tem - ber. . . .

Summer is in bones.
Cock-robin's at Caracas.
Make o, make o, make o,
Oto - otu - bre.

And the rude leaves fall.
The rain falls. The sky
Falls and lies with the worms.
The street lamps

Are those that have been hanged,
Dangling in an illogical
To and to and fro
Fro Niz - nil - imbo.

CONTRARY THESES (I)

Now grapes are plush upon the vines.
A soldier walks before my door.

The hives are heavy with the combs.
Before, before, before my door.

And seraphs cluster on the domes,
And saints are brilliant in fresh cloaks.

Before, before, before my door.
The shadows lessen on the walls.

The bareness of the house returns.
An acid sunlight fills the halls.

Before, before. Blood smears the oaks.
A soldier stalks before my door.

PHOSPHOR READING BY HIS OWN LIGHT

It is difficult to read. The page is dark.
Yet he knows what it is that he expects.

The page is blank or a frame without a glass
Or a glass that is empty when he looks.

The greenness of night lies on the page and goes
Down deeply in the empty glass . . .

Look, realist, not knowing what you expect.
The green falls on you as you look,

Falls on and makes and gives, even a speech.
And you think that that is what you expect,

That elemental parent, the green night,
Teaching a fusky alphabet.

CONTRARY THESES (II)

One chemical afternoon in mid-autumn,
When the grand mechanics of earth and sky were near,
Even the leaves of the locust were yellow then,

He walked with his year-old boy on his shoulder.
The sun shone and the dog barked and the baby slept.
The leaves, even of the locust, the green locust.

He wanted and looked for a final refuge,
From the bombastic intimations of winter
And the martyrs à la mode. He walked toward

An abstract, of which the sun, the dog, the boy
Were contours. Cold was chilling the wide-moving swans.
The leaves were falling like notes from a piano.

The abstract was suddenly there and gone again.
The negroes were playing football in the park.
The abstract that he saw, like the locust-leaves, plainly:

The premiss from which all things were conclusions,
The noble, Alexandrine verve. The flies
And the bees still sought the chrysanthemums' odor.

GOD IS GOOD. IT IS A BEAUTIFUL NIGHT

Look round, brown moon, brown bird, as you rise to fly,
Look round at the head and zither
On the ground.

Look round you as you start to rise, brown moon,
At the book and shoe, the rotted rose
At the door.

This was the place to which you came last night,
Flew close to, flew to without rising away.
Now, again,

In your light, the head is speaking. It reads the book.
It becomes the scholar again, seeking celestial
Rendezvous,

Picking thin music on the rustiest string,
Squeezing the reddest fragrance from the stump
Of summer.

The venerable song falls from your fiery wings.
The song of the great space of your age pierces
The fresh night.

THE MOTIVE FOR METAPHOR

You like it under the trees in autumn,
Because everything is half dead.
The wind moves like a cripple among the leaves
And repeats words without meaning.

In the same way, you were happy in spring,
With the half colors of quarter-things,
The slightly brighter sky, the melting clouds,
The single bird, the obscure moon—

The obscure moon lighting an obscure world
Of things that would never be quite expressed,
Where you yourself were never quite yourself
And did not want nor have to be,

Desiring the exhilarations of changes:
The motive for metaphor, shrinking from
The weight of primary noon,
The A B C of being,

The ruddy temper, the hammer
Of red and blue, the hard sound—
Steel against intimation—the sharp flash,
The vital, arrogant, fatal, dominant X.

NO POSSUM, NO SOP, NO TATERS

He is not here, the old sun,
As absent as if we were asleep.

The field is frozen. The leaves are dry.
Bad is final in this light.

In this bleak air the broken stalks
Have arms without hands. They have trunks

Without legs or, for that, without heads.
They have heads in which a captive cry

Is merely the moving of a tongue.
Snow sparkles like eyesight falling to earth,

Like seeing fallen brightly away.
The leaves hop, scraping on the ground.

It is deep January. The sky is hard.
The stalks are firmly rooted in ice.

It is in this solitude, a syllable,
Out of these gawky flitterings,

Intones its single emptiness,
The savagest hollow of winter-sound.

It is here, in this bad, that we reach
The last purity of the knowledge of good.

The crow looks rusty as he rises up.
Bright is the malice in his eye . . .

One joins him there for company,
But at a distance, in another tree.

SO-AND-SO RECLINING ON HER COUCH

On her side, reclining on her elbow.
This mechanism, this apparition,
Suppose we call it Projection A.

She floats in air at the level of
The eye, completely anonymous,
Born, as she was, at twenty-one,

Without lineage or language, only
The curving of her hip, as motionless gesture,
Eyes dripping blue, so much to learn.

If just above her head there hung,
Suspended in air, the slightest crown
Of Gothic prong and practick bright,

The suspension, as in solid space,
The suspending hand withdrawn, would be
An invisible gesture. Let this be called

Projection B. To get at the thing
Without gestures is to get at it as
Idea. She floats in the contention, the flux

Between the thing as idea and
The idea as thing. She is half who made her.
This is the final Projection, C.

The arrangement contains the desire of
The artist. But one confides in what has no
Concealed creator. One walks easily

The unpainted shore, accepts the world
As anything but sculpture. Good-bye,
Mrs. Pappadopoulos, and thanks.

SOMNAMBULISMA

On an old shore, the vulgar ocean rolls
Noiselessly, noiselessly, resembling a thin bird,
That thinks of settling, yet never settles, on a nest.

The wings keep spreading and yet are never wings.
The claws keep scratching on the shale, the shallow shale,
The sounding shallow, until by water washed away.

The generations of the bird are all
By water washed away. They follow after.
They follow, follow, follow, in water washed away.

Without this bird that never settles, without
Its generations that follow in their universe,
The ocean, falling and falling on the hollow shore,

Would be a geography of the dead: not of that land
To which they may have gone, but of the place in which
They lived, in which they lacked a pervasive being,

In which no scholar, separately dwelling,
Poured forth the fine fins, the gawky beaks, the personalia,
Which, as a man feeling everything, were his.

CRUDE FOYER

Thought is false happiness: the idea
That merely by thinking one can,
Or may, penetrate, not may,
But can, that one is sure to be able—

That there lies at the end of thought
A foyer of the spirit in a landscape
Of the mind, in which we sit
And wear humanity's bleak crown;

In which we read the critique of paradise
And say it is the work
Of a comedian, this critique;
In which we sit and breathe

An innocence of an absolute,
False happiness, since we know that we use
Only the eye as faculty, that the mind
Is the eye, and that this landscape of the mind

Is a landscape only of the eye; and that
We are ignorant men incapable
Of the least, minor, vital metaphor, content,
At last, there, when it turns out to be here.

THE CREATIONS OF SOUND

If the poetry of *X* was music,
So that it came to him of its own,
Without understanding, out of the wall

Or in the ceiling, in sounds not chosen,
Or chosen quickly, in a freedom
That was their element, we should not know

That *X* is an obstruction, a man
Too exactly himself, and that there are words
Better without an author, without a poet,

Or having a separate author, a different poet,
An accretion from ourselves, intelligent
Beyond intelligence, an artificial man

At a distance, a secondary expositor,
A being of sound, whom one does not approach
Through any exaggeration. From him, we collect.

Tell *X* that speech is not dirty silence
Clarified. It is silence made still dirtier.
It is more than an imitation for the ear.

He lacks this venerable complication.
His poems are not of the second part of life.
They do not make the visible a little hard

To see nor, reverberating, eke out the mind
On peculiar horns, themselves eked out
By the spontaneous particulars of sound.

We do not say ourselves like that in poems.
We say ourselves in syllables that rise
From the floor, rising in speech we do not speak.

HOLIDAY IN REALITY

I

It was something to see that their white was different,
Sharp as white paint in the January sun;

Something to feel that they needed another yellow,
Less Aix than Stockholm, hardly a yellow at all,

A vibrancy not to be taken for granted, from
A sun in an almost colorless, cold heaven.

They had known that there was not even a common speech,
Palabra of a common man who did not exist.

Why should they not know they had everything of their own
As each had a particular woman and her touch?

After all, they knew that to be real each had
To find for himself his earth, his sky, his sea.

And the words for them and the colors that they possessed.
It was impossible to breathe at Durand-Ruel's.

II

The flowering Judas grows from the belly or not at all.
The breast is covered with violets. It is a green leaf.

Spring is umbilical or else it is not spring.
Spring is the truth of spring or nothing, a waste, a fake.

These trees and their argentines, their dark-spiced branches,
Grow out of the spirit or they are fantastic dust.

The bud of the apple is desire, the down-falling gold,
The catbird's gobble in the morning half-awake—

These are real only if I make them so. Whistle
For me, grow green for me and, as you whistle and grow green,

Intangible arrows quiver and stick in the skin
And I taste at the root of the tongue the unreal of what is real.

ESTHÉTIQUE DU MAL

I

He was at Naples writing letters home
And, between his letters, reading paragraphs
On the sublime. Vesuvius had groaned
For a month. It was pleasant to be sitting there,
While the sultriest fulgurations, flickering,
Cast corners in the glass. He could describe
The terror of the sound because the sound
Was ancient. He tried to remember the phrases: pain
Audible at noon, pain torturing itself,
Pain killing pain on the very point of pain.
The volcano trembled in another ether,
As the body trembles at the end of life.

It was almost time for lunch. Pain is human.
There were roses in the cool café. His book
Made sure of the most correct catastrophe.
Except for us, Vesuvius might consume
In solid fire the utmost earth and know
No pain (ignoring the cocks that crow us up
To die). This is a part of the sublime
From which we shrink. And yet, except for us,
The total past felt nothing when destroyed.

II

At a town in which acacias grew, he lay
On his balcony at night. Warblings became
Too dark, too far, too much the accents of
Afflicted sleep, too much the syllables
That would form themselves, in time, and communicate
The intelligence of his despair, express
What meditation never quite achieved.

The moon rose up as if it had escaped
His meditation. It evaded his mind.
It was part of a supremacy always
Above him. The moon was always free from him,
As night was free from him. The shadow touched
Or merely seemed to touch him as he spoke
A kind of elegy he found in space:

It is pain that is indifferent to the sky
In spite of the yellow of the acacias, the scent
Of them in the air still hanging heavily
In the hoary-hanging night. It does not regard
This freedom, this supremacy, and in
Its own hallucination never sees
How that which rejects it saves it in the end.

III

His firm stanzas hang like hives in hell
Or what hell was, since now both heaven and hell
Are one, and here, O terra infidel.

The fault lies with an over-human god,
Who by sympathy has made himself a man
And is not to be distinguished, when we cry

Because we suffer, our oldest parent, peer
Of the populace of the heart, the reddest lord,
Who has gone before us in experience.

If only he would not pity us so much,
Weaken our fate, relieve us of woe both great
And small, a constant fellow of destiny,

A too, too human god, self-pity's kin
And uncourageous genesis . . . It seems
As if the health of the world might be enough.

It seems as if the honey of common summer
Might be enough, as if the golden combs
Were part of a sustenance itself enough,

As if hell, so modified, had disappeared,
As if pain, no longer satanic mimicry,
Could be borne, as if we were sure to find our way.

IV

Livre de Toutes Sortes de Fleurs d'après Nature.
All sorts of flowers. That's the sentimentalist.
When B. sat down at the piano and made
A transparence in which we heard music, made music,
In which we heard transparent sounds, did he play
All sorts of notes? Or did he play only one
In an ecstasy of its associates,
Variations in the tones of a single sound,
The last, or sounds so single they seemed one?

And then that Spaniard of the rose, itself
Hot-hooded and dark-blooded, rescued the rose
From nature, each time he saw it, making it,
As he saw it, exist in his own especial eye.
Can we conceive of him as rescuing less,
As muffing the mistress for her several maids,
As foregoing the nakedest passion for barefoot
Philandering? . . . The genius of misfortune
Is not a sentimentalist. He is
That evil, that evil in the self, from which
In desperate hallow, rugged gesture, fault

Falls out on everything: the genius of
The mind, which is our being, wrong and wrong,
The genius of the body, which is our world,
Spent in the false engagements of the mind.

v

Softly let all true sympathizers come,
Without the inventions of sorrow or the sob
Beyond invention. Within what we permit,
Within the actual, the warm, the near,
So great a unity, that it is bliss,
Ties us to those we love. For this familiar,
This brother even in the father's eye,
This brother half-spoken in the mother's throat
And these regalia, these things disclosed,
These nebulous brilliancies in the smallest look
Of the being's deepest darling, we forego
Lament, willingly forfeit the ai-ai

Of parades in the obscurer selvages.
Be near me, come closer, touch my hand, phrases
Compounded of dear relation, spoken twice,
Once by the lips, once by the services
Of central sense, these minutiae mean more
Than clouds, benevolences, distant heads.
These are within what we permit, in-bar
Exquisite in poverty against the suns
Of ex-bar, in-bar retaining attributes
With which we vested, once, the golden forms
And the damasked memory of the golden forms
And ex-bar's flower and fire of the festivals
Of the damasked memory of the golden forms,
Before we were wholly human and knew ourselves.

VI

The sun, in clownish yellow, but not a clown,
Brings the day to perfection and then fails. He dwells
In a consummate prime, yet still desires
A further consummation. For the lunar month
He makes the tenderest research, intent
On a transmutation which, when seen, appears
To be askew. And space is filled with his
Rejected years. A big bird pecks at him
For food. The big bird's boney appetite
Is as insatiable as the sun's. The bird
Rose from an imperfection of its own
To feed on the yellow bloom of the yellow fruit
Dropped down from turquoise leaves. In the landscape of
The sun, its grossest appetite becomes less gross,
Yet, when corrected, has its curious lapses,
Its glitters, its divinations of serene
Indulgence out of all celestial sight.

The sun is the country wherever he is. The bird
In the brightest landscape downwardly revolves
Disdaining each astringent ripening,
Evading the point of redness, not content
To repose in an hour or season or long era
Of the country colors crowding against it, since
The yellow grassman's mind is still immense,
Still promises perfections cast away.

VII

How red the rose that is the soldier's wound,
The wounds of many soldiers, the wounds of all
The soldiers that have fallen, red in blood,
The soldier of time grown deathless in great size.

A mountain in which no ease is ever found,
Unless indifference to deeper death
Is ease, stands in the dark, a shadows' hill,
And there the soldier of time has deathless rest.

Concentric circles of shadows, motionless
Of their own part, yet moving on the wind,
Form mystical convolutions in the sleep
Of time's red soldier deathless on his bed.

The shadows of his fellows ring him round
In the high night, the summer breathes for them
Its fragrance, a heavy somnolence, and for him,
For the soldier of time, it breathes a summer sleep,

In which his wound is good because life was.
No part of him was ever part of death.
A woman smoothes her forehead with her hand
And the soldier of time lies calm beneath that stroke.

VIII

The death of Satan was a tragedy
For the imagination. A capital
Negation destroyed him in his tenement
And, with him, many blue phenomena.
It was not the end he had foreseen. He knew
That his revenge created filial
Revenges. And negation was eccentric.
It had nothing of the Julian thunder-cloud:
The assassin flash and rumble . . . He was denied.
Phantoms, what have you left? What underground?
What place in which to be is not enough

To be? You go, poor phantoms, without place
Like silver in the sheathing of the sight,
As the eye closes . . . How cold the vacancy
When the phantoms are gone and the shaken realist
First sees reality. The mortal no
Has its emptiness and tragic expirations.
The tragedy, however, may have begun,
Again, in the imagination's new beginning,
In the yes of the realist spoken because he must
Say yes, spoken because under every no
Lay a passion for yes that had never been broken.

IX

Panic in the face of the moon—round effendi
Or the phosphored sleep in which he walks abroad
Or the majolica dish heaped up with phosphored fruit
That he sends ahead, out of the goodness of his heart,
To anyone that comes—panic, because
The moon is no longer these nor anything
And nothing is left but comic ugliness
Or a lustred nothingness. Effendi, he
That has lost the folly of the moon becomes
The prince of the proverbs of pure poverty.
To lose sensibility, to see what one sees,
As if sight had not its own miraculous thrift,
To hear only what one hears, one meaning alone,
As if the paradise of meaning ceased
To be paradise, it is this to be destitute.
This is the sky divested of its fountains.
Here in the west indifferent crickets chant
Through our indifferent crises. Yet we require
Another chant, an incantation, as in
Another and later genesis, music

That buffets the shapes of its possible halcyon
Against the haggardie . . . A loud, large water
Bubbles up in the night and drowns the crickets' sound.
It is a declaration, a primitive ecstasy,
Truth's favors sonorously exhibited.

                X

He had studied the nostalgias. In these
He sought the most grossly maternal, the creature
Who most fecundly assuaged him, the softest
Woman with a vague moustache and not the mauve
Maman. His anima liked its animal
And liked it unsubjugated, so that home
Was a return to birth, a being born
Again in the savagest severity,
Desiring fiercely, the child of a mother fierce
In his body, fiercer in his mind, merciless
To accomplish the truth in his intelligence.
It is true there were other mothers, singular
In form, lovers of heaven and earth, she-wolves
And forest tigresses and women mixed
With the sea. These were fantastic. There were homes
Like things submerged with their englutted sounds,
That were never wholly still. The softest woman,
Because she is as she was, reality,
The gross, the fecund, proved him against the touch
Of impersonal pain. Reality explained.
It was the last nostalgia: that he
Should understand. That he might suffer or that
He might die was the innocence of living, if life
Itself was innocent. To say that it was
Disentangled him from sleek ensolacings.

XI

Life is a bitter aspic. We are not
At the center of a diamond. At dawn,
The paratroopers fall and as they fall
They mow the lawn. A vessel sinks in waves
Of people, as big bell-billows from its bell
Bell-bellow in the village steeple. Violets,
Great tufts, spring up from buried houses
Of poor, dishonest people, for whom the steeple,
Long since, rang out farewell, farewell, farewell.

Natives of poverty, children of malheur,
The gaiety of language is our seigneur.

A man of bitter appetite despises
A well-made scene in which paratroopers
Select adieux; and he despises this:
A ship that rolls on a confected ocean,
The weather pink, the wind in motion; and this:
A steeple that tip-tops the classic sun's
Arrangements; and the violets' exhumo.

The tongue caresses these exacerbations.
They press it as epicure, distinguishing
Themselves from its essential savor,
Like hunger that feeds on its own hungriness.

XII

He disposes the world in categories, thus:
The peopled and the unpeopled. In both, he is
Alone. But in the peopled world, there is,
Besides the people, his knowledge of them. In
The unpeopled, there is his knowledge of himself.
Which is more desperate in the moments when
The will demands that what he thinks be true?

Is it himself in them that he knows or they
In him? If it is himself in them, they have
No secret from him. If it is they in him,
He has no secret from them. This knowledge
Of them and of himself destroys both worlds,
Except when he escapes from it. To be
Alone is not to know them or himself.

This creates a third world without knowledge,
In which no one peers, in which the will makes no
Demands. It accepts whatever is as true,
Including pain, which, otherwise, is false.
In the third world, then, there is no pain. Yes, but
What lover has one in such rocks, what woman,
However known, at the center of the heart?

        XIII

It may be that one life is a punishment
For another, as the son's life for the father's.
But that concerns the secondary characters.
It is a fragmentary tragedy
Within the universal whole. The son
And the father alike and equally are spent,
Each one, by the necessity of being
Himself, the unalterable necessity
Of being this unalterable animal.
This force of nature in action is the major
Tragedy. This is destiny unperplexed,
The happiest enemy. And it may be
That in his Mediterranean cloister a man,
Reclining, eased of desire, establishes
The visible, a zone of blue and orange
Versicolorings, establishes a time

To watch the fire-feinting sea and calls it good,
The ultimate good, sure of a reality
Of the longest meditation, the maximum,
The assassin's scene. Evil in evil is
Comparative. The assassin discloses himself,
The force that destroys us is disclosed, within
This maximum, an adventure to be endured
With the politest helplessness. Ay-mi!
One feels its action moving in the blood.

XIV

Victor Serge said, "I followed his argument
With the blank uneasiness which one might feel
In the presence of a logical lunatic."
He said it of Konstantinov. Revolution
Is the affair of logical lunatics.
The politics of emotion must appear
To be an intellectual structure. The cause
Creates a logic not to be distinguished
From lunacy . . . One wants to be able to walk
By the lake at Geneva and consider logic:
To think of the logicians in their graves
And of the worlds of logic in their great tombs.
Lakes are more reasonable than oceans. Hence,
A promenade amid the grandeurs of the mind,
By a lake, with clouds like lights among great tombs,
Gives one a blank uneasiness, as if
One might meet Konstantinov, who would interrupt
With his lunacy. He would not be aware of the lake.
He would be the lunatic of one idea
In a world of ideas, who would have all the people
Live, work, suffer and die in that idea
In a world of ideas. He would not be aware of the clouds,
Lighting the martyrs of logic with white fire.
His extreme of logic would be illogical.

XV

The greatest poverty is not to live
In a physical world, to feel that one's desire
Is too difficult to tell from despair. Perhaps,
After death, the non-physical people, in paradise,
Itself non-physical, may, by chance, observe
The green corn gleaming and experience
The minor of what we feel. The adventurer
In humanity has not conceived of a race
Completely physical in a physical world.
The green corn gleams and the metaphysicals
Lie sprawling in majors of the August heat,
The rotund emotions, paradise unknown.

This is the thesis scrivened in delight,
The reverberating psalm, the right chorale.

One might have thought of sight, but who could think
Of what it sees, for all the ill it sees?
Speech found the ear, for all the evil sound,
But the dark italics it could not propound.
And out of what one sees and hears and out
Of what one feels, who could have thought to make
So many selves, so many sensuous worlds,
As if the air, the mid-day air, was swarming
With the metaphysical changes that occur,
Merely in living as and where we live.

THE BED OF OLD JOHN ZELLER

This structure of ideas, these ghostly sequences
Of the mind, result only in disaster. It follows,
Casual poet, that to add your own disorder to disaster

Makes more of it. It is easy to wish for another structure
Of ideas and to say as usual that there must be
Other ghostly sequences and, it would be, luminous

Sequences, thought of among spheres in the old peak of night:
This is the habit of wishing, as if one's grandfather lay
In one's heart and wished as he had always wished, unable

To sleep in that bed for its disorder, talking of ghostly
Sequences that would be sleep and ting-tang tossing, so that
He might slowly forget. It is more difficult to evade

That habit of wishing and to accept the structure
Of things as the structure of ideas. It was the structure
Of things at least that was thought of in the old peak of night.

LESS AND LESS HUMAN, O SAVAGE SPIRIT

If there must be a god in the house, must be,
Saying things in the rooms and on the stair,

Let him move as the sunlight moves on the floor,
Or moonlight, silently, as Plato's ghost

Or Aristotle's skeleton. Let him hang out
His stars on the wall. He must dwell quietly.

He must be incapable of speaking, closed,
As those are: as light, for all its motion, is;

As color, even the closest to us, is;
As shapes, though they portend us, are.

It is the human that is the alien,
The human that has no cousin in the moon.

It is the human that demands his speech
From beasts or from the incommunicable mass.

If there must be a god in the house, let him be one
That will not hear us when we speak: a coolness,

A vermilioned nothingness, any stick of the mass
Of which we are too distantly a part.

FLYER'S FALL

This man escaped the dirty fates,
Knowing that he did nobly, as he died.

Darkness, nothingness of human after-death,
Receive and keep him in the deepnesses of space—

Profundum, physical thunder, dimension in which
We believe without belief, beyond belief.

DEBRIS OF LIFE AND MIND

There is so little that is close and warm.
It is as if we were never children.

Sit in the room. It is true in the moonlight
That it is as if we had never been young.

We ought not to be awake. It is from this
That a bright red woman will be rising

And, standing in violent golds, will brush her hair.
She will speak thoughtfully the words of a line.

She will think about them not quite able to sing.
Besides, when the sky is so blue, things sing themselves,

Even for her, already for her. She will listen
And feel that her color is a meditation,

The most gay and yet not so gay as it was.
Stay here. Speak of familiar things a while.

DESCRIPTION WITHOUT PLACE

I

It is possible that to seem—it is to be,
As the sun is something seeming and it is.

The sun is an example. What it seems
It is and in such seeming all things are.

Thus things are like a seeming of the sun
Or like a seeming of the moon or night

Or sleep. It was a queen that made it seem
By the illustrious nothing of her name.

Her green mind made the world around her green.
The queen is an example . . . This green queen

In the seeming of the summer of her sun
By her own seeming made the summer change.

In the golden vacancy she came, and comes,
And seems to be on the saying of her name.

Her time becomes again, as it became,
The crown and week-day coronal of her fame.

II

Such seemings are the actual ones: the way
Things look each day, each morning, or the style

Peculiar to the queen, this queen or that,
The lesser seeming original in the blind

Forward of the eye that, in its backward, sees
The greater seeming of the major mind.

An age is a manner collected from a queen.
An age is green or red. An age believes

Or it denies. An age is solitude
Or a barricade against the singular man

By the incalculably plural. Hence
Its identity is merely a thing that seems,

In the seeming of an original in the eye,
In the major manner of a queen, the green,

The red, the blue, the argent queen. If not,
What subtlety would apparition have?

In flat appearance we should be and be,
Except for delicate clinkings not explained.

These are the actual seemings that we see,
Hear, feel and know. We feel and know them so.

    III

There are potential seemings, arrogant
To be, as on the youngest poet's page,

Or in the dark musician, listening
To hear more brightly the contriving chords.

There are potential seemings turbulent
In the death of a soldier, like the utmost will,

The more than human commonplace of blood,
The breath that gushes upward and is gone,

And another breath emerging out of death,
That speaks for him such seemings as death gives.

There might be, too, a change immenser than
A poet's metaphors in which being would

Come true, a point in the fire of music where
Dazzle yields to a clarity and we observe,

And observing is completing and we are content,
In a world that shrinks to an immediate whole,

That we do not need to understand, complete
Without secret arrangements of it in the mind.

There might be in the curling-out of spring
A purple-leaping element that forth

Would froth the whole heaven with its seeming-so,
The intentions of a mind as yet unknown,

The spirit of one dwelling in a seed,
Itself that seed's ripe, unpredictable fruit.

Things are as they seemed to Calvin or to Anne
Of England, to Pablo Neruda in Ceylon,

To Nietzsche in Basel, to Lenin by a lake.
But the integrations of the past are like

A *Museo Olimpico*, so much
So little, our affair, which is the affair

Of the possible: seemings that are to be,
Seemings that it is possible may be.

IV

Nietzsche in Basel studied the deep pool
Of these discolorations, mastering

The moving and the moving of their forms
In the much-mottled motion of blank time.

His revery was the deepness of the pool,
The very pool, his thoughts the colored forms,

The eccentric souvenirs of human shapes,
Wrapped in their seemings, crowd on curious crowd,

In a kind of total affluence, all first,
All final, colors subjected in revery

To an innate grandiose, an innate light,
The sun of Nietzsche gildering the pool,

Yes: gildering the swarm-like manias
In perpetual revolution, round and round . . .

Lenin on a bench beside a lake disturbed
The swans. He was not the man for swans.

The slouch of his body and his look were not
In suavest keeping. The shoes, the clothes, the hat

Suited the decadence of those silences,
In which he sat. All chariots were drowned. The swans

Moved on the buried water where they lay.
Lenin took bread from his pocket, scattered it—

The swans fled outward to remoter reaches,
As if they knew of distant beaches; and were

Dissolved. The distances of space and time
Were one and swans far off were swans to come.

The eye of Lenin kept the far-off shapes.
His mind raised up, down-drowned, the chariots.

And reaches, beaches, tomorrow's regions became
One thinking of apocalyptic legions.

V

If seeming is description without place,
The spirit's universe, then a summer's day,

Even the seeming of a summer's day,
Is description without place. It is a sense

To which we refer experience, a knowledge
Incognito, the column in the desert,

On which the dove alights. Description is
Composed of a sight indifferent to the eye.

It is an expectation, a desire,
A palm that rises up beyond the sea,

A little different from reality:
The difference that we make in what we see

And our memorials of that difference,
Sprinklings of bright particulars from the sky.

The future is description without place,
The categorical predicate, the arc.

It is a wizened starlight growing young,
In which old stars are planets of morning, fresh

In the brilliantest descriptions of new day,
Before it comes, the just anticipation

Of the appropriate creatures, jubilant,
The forms that are attentive in thin air.

     VI

Description is revelation. It is not
The thing described, nor false facsimile.

It is an artificial thing that exists,
In its own seeming, plainly visible,

Yet not too closely the double of our lives,
Intenser than any actual life could be,

A text we should be born that we might read,
More explicit than the experience of sun

And moon, the book of reconciliation,
Book of a concept only possible

In description, canon central in itself,
The thesis of the plentifullest John.

VII

Thus the theory of description matters most.
It is the theory of the word for those

For whom the word is the making of the world,
The buzzing world and lisping firmament.

It is a world of words to the end of it,
In which nothing solid is its solid self.

As, men make themselves their speech: the hard hidalgo
Lives in the mountainous character of his speech;

And in that mountainous mirror Spain acquires
The knowledge of Spain and of the hidalgo's hat—

A seeming of the Spaniard, a style of life,
The invention of a nation in a phrase,

In a description hollowed out of hollow-bright,
The artificer of subjects still half night.

It matters, because everything we say
Of the past is description without place, a cast

Of the imagination, made in sound;
And because what we say of the future must portend,

Be alive with its own seemings, seeming to be
Like rubies reddened by rubies reddening.

LATE HYMN FROM THE MYRRH-MOUNTAIN

Unsnack your snood, madanna, for the stars
Are shining on all brows of Neversink.

Already the green bird of summer has flown
Away. The night-flies acknowledge these planets,

Predestined to this night, this noise and the place
Of summer. Tomorrow will look like today,

Will appear like it. But it will be an appearance,
A shape left behind, with like wings spreading out,

Brightly empowered with like colors, swarmingly,
But not quite molten, not quite the fluid thing,

A little changed by tips of artifice, changed
By the glints of sound from the grass. These are not

The early constellations, from which came the first
Illustrious intimations—uncertain love,

The knowledge of being, sense without sense of time.
Take the diamonds from your hair and lay them down.

The deer-grass is thin. The timothy is brown.
The shadow of an external world comes near.

MAN CARRYING THING

The poem must resist the intelligence
Almost successfully. Illustration:

A brune figure in winter evening resists
Identity. The thing he carries resists

The most necessitous sense. Accept them, then,
As secondary (parts not quite perceived

Of the obvious whole, uncertain particles
Of the certain solid, the primary free from doubt,

Things floating like the first hundred flakes of snow
Out of a storm we must endure all night,

Out of a storm of secondary things),
A horror of thoughts that suddenly are real.

We must endure our thoughts all night, until
The bright obvious stands motionless in cold.

CHAOS IN MOTION AND NOT IN MOTION

Oh, that this lashing wind was something more
Than the spirit of Ludwig Richter . . .

The rain is pouring down. It is July.
There is lightning and the thickest thunder.

It is a spectacle. Scene 10 becomes 11,
In Series X, Act IV, et cetera.

People fall out of windows, trees tumble down,
Summer is changed to winter, the young grow old,

The air is full of children, statues, roofs
And snow. The theatre is spinning round,

Colliding with deaf-mute churches and optical trains.
The most massive sopranos are singing songs of scales.

And Ludwig Richter, turbulent Schlemihl,
Has lost the whole in which he was contained,

Knows desire without an object of desire,
All mind and violence and nothing felt.

He knows he has nothing more to think about,
Like the wind that lashes everything at once.

THE HOUSE WAS QUIET AND THE WORLD WAS CALM

The house was quiet and the world was calm.
The reader became the book; and summer night

Was like the conscious being of the book.
The house was quiet and the world was calm.

The words were spoken as if there was no book,
Except that the reader leaned above the page,

Wanted to lean, wanted much most to be
The scholar to whom his book is true, to whom

The summer night is like a perfection of thought.
The house was quiet because it had to be.

The quiet was part of the meaning, part of the mind:
The access of perfection to the page.

And the world was calm. The truth in a calm world,
In which there is no other meaning, itself

Is calm, itself is summer and night, itself
Is the reader leaning late and reading there.

BURGHERS OF PETTY DEATH

These two by the stone wall
Are a slight part of death.
The grass is still green.

But there is a total death,
A devastation, a death of great height
And depth, covering all surfaces,
Filling the mind.

These are the small townsmen of death,
A man and a woman, like two leaves
That keep clinging to a tree,
Before winter freezes and grows black—

Of great height and depth
Without any feeling, an imperium of quiet,
In which a wasted figure, with an instrument,
Propounds blank final music.

THE RED FERN

The large-leaved day grows rapidly,
And opens in this familiar spot
Its unfamiliar, difficult fern,
Pushing and pushing red after red.

There are doubles of this fern in clouds,
Less firm than the paternal flame,
Yet drenched with its identity,
Reflections and off-shoots, mimic-motes

And mist-mites, dangling seconds, grown
Beyond relation to the parent trunk:
The dazzling, bulging, brightest core,
The furiously burning father-fire . . .

Infant, it is enough in life
To speak of what you see. But wait
Until sight wakens the sleepy eye
And pierces the physical fix of things.

THE DOVE IN THE BELLY

The whole of appearance is a toy. For this,
The dove in the belly builds his nest and coos,

Selah, tempestuous bird. How is it that
The rivers shine and hold their mirrors up,

Like excellence collecting excellence?
How is it that the wooden trees stand up

And live and heap their panniers of green
And hold them round the sultry day? Why should

These mountains being high be, also, bright,
Fetched up with snow that never falls to earth?

And this great esplanade of corn, miles wide,
Is something wished for made effectual

And something more. And the people in costumes,
Though poor, though raggeder than ruin, have that

Within them right for terraces—oh, brave salut!
Deep dove, placate you in your hiddenness.

CREDENCES OF SUMMER

I

Now in midsummer come and all fools slaughtered
And spring's infuriations over and a long way
To the first autumnal inhalations, young broods
Are in the grass, the roses are heavy with a weight
Of fragrance and the mind lays by its trouble.

Now the mind lays by its trouble and considers.
The fidgets of remembrance come to this.
This is the last day of a certain year
Beyond which there is nothing left of time.
It comes to this and the imagination's life.

There is nothing more inscribed nor thought nor felt
And this must comfort the heart's core against
Its false disasters—these fathers standing round,
These mothers touching, speaking, being near,
These lovers waiting in the soft dry grass.

II

Postpone the anatomy of summer, as
The physical pine, the metaphysical pine.
Let's see the very thing and nothing else.
Let's see it with the hottest fire of sight.
Burn everything not part of it to ash.

Trace the gold sun about the whitened sky
Without evasion by a single metaphor.
Look at it in its essential barrenness
And say this, this is the center that I seek.
Fix it in an eternal foliage

And fill the foliage with arrested peace,
Joy of such permanence, right ignorance
Of change still possible. Exile desire
For what is not. This is the barrenness
Of the fertile thing that can attain no more.

III

It is the natural tower of all the world,
The point of survey, green's green apogee,
But a tower more precious than the view beyond,
A point of survey squatting like a throne,
Axis of everything, green's apogee

And happiest folk-land, mostly marriage-hymns.
It is the mountain on which the tower stands,
It is the final mountain. Here the sun,
Sleepless, inhales his proper air, and rests.
This is the refuge that the end creates.

It is the old man standing on the tower,
Who reads no book. His ruddy ancientness
Absorbs the ruddy summer and is appeased,
By an understanding that fulfils his age,
By a feeling capable of nothing more.

IV

One of the limits of reality
Presents itself in Oley when the hay,
Baked through long days, is piled in mows. It is
A land too ripe for enigmas, too serene.
There the distant fails the clairvoyant eye

And the secondary senses of the ear
Swarm, not with secondary sounds, but choirs,
Not evocations but last choirs, last sounds
With nothing else compounded, carried full,
Pure rhetoric of a language without words.

Things stop in that direction and since they stop
The direction stops and we accept what is
As good. The utmost must be good and is
And is our fortune and honey hived in the trees
And mingling of colors at a festival.

V

One day enriches a year. One woman makes
The rest look down. One man becomes a race,
Lofty like him, like him perpetual.
Or do the other days enrich the one?
And is the queen humble as she seems to be,

The charitable majesty of her whole kin?
The bristling soldier, weather-foxed, who looms
In the sunshine is a filial form and one
Of the land's children, easily born, its flesh,
Not fustian. The more than casual blue

Contains the year and other years and hymns
And people, without souvenir. The day
Enriches the year, not as embellishment.
Stripped of remembrance, it displays its strength—
The youth, the vital son, the heroic power.

VI

The rock cannot be broken. It is the truth.
It rises from land and sea and covers them.
It is a mountain half way green and then,
The other immeasurable half, such rock
As placid air becomes. But it is not

A hermit's truth nor symbol in hermitage.
It is the visible rock, the audible,
The brilliant mercy of a sure repose,
On this present ground, the vividest repose,
Things certain sustaining us in certainty.

It is the rock of summer, the extreme,
A mountain luminous half way in bloom
And then half way in the extremest light
Of sapphires flashing from the central sky,
As if twelve princes sat before a king.

VII

Far in the woods they sang their unreal songs,
Secure. It was difficult to sing in face
Of the object. The singers had to avert themselves
Or else avert the object. Deep in the woods
They sang of summer in the common fields.

They sang desiring an object that was near,
In face of which desire no longer moved,
Nor made of itself that which it could not find . . .
Three times the concentered self takes hold, three times
The thrice concentered self, having possessed

The object, grips it in savage scrutiny,
Once to make captive, once to subjugate
Or yield to subjugation, once to proclaim
The meaning of the capture, this hard prize,
Fully made, fully apparent, fully found.

VIII

The trumpet of morning blows in the clouds and through
The sky. It is the visible announced,
It is the more than visible, the more
Than sharp, illustrious scene. The trumpet cries
This is the successor of the invisible.

This is its substitute in stratagems
Of the spirit. This, in sight and memory,
Must take its place, as what is possible
Replaces what is not. The resounding cry
Is like ten thousand tumblers tumbling down

To share the day. The trumpet supposes that
A mind exists, aware of division, aware
Of its cry as clarion, its diction's way
As that of a personage in a multitude:
Man's mind grown venerable in the unreal.

Fly low, cock bright, and stop on a bean pole. Let
Your brown breast redden, while you wait for warmth.
With one eye watch the willow, motionless.
The gardener's cat is dead, the gardener gone
And last year's garden grows salacious weeds.

A complex of emotions falls apart,
In an abandoned spot. Soft, civil bird,
The decay that you regard: of the arranged
And of the spirit of the arranged, *douceurs,*
Tristesses, the fund of life and death, suave bush

And polished beast, this complex falls apart.
And on your bean pole, it may be, you detect
Another complex of other emotions, not
So soft, so civil, and you make a sound,
Which is not part of the listener's own sense.

The personae of summer play the characters
Of an inhuman author, who meditates
With the gold bugs, in blue meadows, late at night.
He does not hear his characters talk. He sees
Them mottled, in the moodiest costumes,

Of blue and yellow, sky and sun, belted
And knotted, sashed and seamed, half pales of red,
Half pales of green, appropriate habit for
The huge decorum, the manner of the time,
Part of the mottled mood of summer's whole,

In which the characters speak because they want
To speak, the fat, the roseate characters,
Free, for a moment, from malice and sudden cry,
Completed in a completed scene, speaking
Their parts as in a youthful happiness.

NOTES TOWARD A SUPREME FICTION

To Henry Church

And for what, except for you, do I feel love?
Do I press the extremest book of the wisest man
Close to me, hidden in me day and night?
In the uncertain light of single, certain truth,
Equal in living changingness to the light
In which I meet you, in which we sit at rest,
For a moment in the central of our being,
The vivid transparence that you bring is peace.

IT MUST BE ABSTRACT

I

Begin, ephebe, by perceiving the idea
Of this invention, this invented world,
The inconceivable idea of the sun.

You must become an ignorant man again
And see the sun again with an ignorant eye
And see it clearly in the idea of it.

Never suppose an inventing mind as source
Of this idea nor for that mind compose
A voluminous master folded in his fire.

How clean the sun when seen in its idea,
Washed in the remotest cleanliness of a heaven
That has expelled us and our images . . .

The death of one god is the death of all.
Let purple Phoebus lie in umber harvest,
Let Phoebus slumber and die in autumn umber,

Phoebus is dead, ephebe. But Phoebus was
A name for something that never could be named.
There was a project for the sun and is.

There is a project for the sun. The sun
Must bear no name, gold flourisher, but be
In the difficulty of what it is to be.

II

It is the celestial ennui of apartments
That sends us back to the first idea, the quick
Of this invention; and yet so poisonous

Are the ravishments of truth, so fatal to
The truth itself, the first idea becomes
The hermit in a poet's metaphors,

Who comes and goes and comes and goes all day.
May there be an ennui of the first idea?
What else, prodigious scholar, should there be?

The monastic man is an artist. The philosopher
Appoints man's place in music, say, today.
But the priest desires. The philosopher desires.

And not to have is the beginning of desire.
To have what is not is its ancient cycle.
It is desire at the end of winter, when

It observes the effortless weather turning blue
And sees the myosotis on its bush.
Being virile, it hears the calendar hymn.

It knows that what it has is what is not
And throws it away like a thing of another time,
As morning throws off stale moonlight and shabby sleep.

III

The poem refreshes life so that we share,
For a moment, the first idea . . . It satisfies
Belief in an immaculate beginning

And sends us, winged by an unconscious will,
To an immaculate end. We move between these points:
From that ever-early candor to its late plural

And the candor of them is the strong exhilaration
Of what we feel from what we think, of thought
Beating in the heart, as if blood newly came,

An elixir, an excitation, a pure power.
The poem, through candor, brings back a power again
That gives a candid kind to everything.

We say: At night an Arabian in my room,
With his damned hoobla-hoobla-hoobla-how,
Inscribes a primitive astronomy

Across the unscrawled fores the future casts
And throws his stars around the floor. By day
The wood-dove used to chant his hoobla-hoo

And still the grossest iridescence of ocean
Howls hoo and rises and howls hoo and falls.
Life's nonsense pierces us with strange relation.

IV

The first idea was not our own. Adam
In Eden was the father of Descartes
And Eve made air the mirror of herself,

Of her sons and of her daughters. They found themselves
In heaven as in a glass; a second earth;
And in the earth itself they found a green—

The inhabitants of a very varnished green.
But the first idea was not to shape the clouds
In imitation. The clouds preceded us.

There was a muddy center before we breathed.
There was a myth before the myth began,
Venerable and articulate and complete.

From this the poem springs: that we live in a place
That is not our own and, much more, not ourselves
And hard it is in spite of blazoned days.

We are the mimics. Clouds are pedagogues.
The air is not a mirror but bare board,
Coulisse bright-dark, tragic chiaroscuro

And comic color of the rose, in which
Abysmal instruments make sounds like pips
Of the sweeping meanings that we add to them.

     V

The lion roars at the enraging desert,
Reddens the sand with his red-colored noise,
Defies red emptiness to evolve his match,

Master by foot and jaws and by the mane,
Most supple challenger. The elephant
Breaches the darkness of Ceylon with blares,

The glitter-goes on surfaces of tanks,
Shattering velvetest far-away. The bear,
The ponderous cinnamon, snarls in his mountain

At summer thunder and sleeps through winter snow.
But you, ephebe, look from your attic window,
Your mansard with a rented piano. You lie

In silence upon your bed. You clutch the corner
Of the pillow in your hand. You writhe and press
A bitter utterance from your writhing, dumb,

Yet voluble of dumb violence. You look
Across the roofs as sigil and as ward
And in your center mark them and are cowed . . .

These are the heroic children whom time breeds
Against the first idea—to lash the lion,
Caparison elephants, teach bears to juggle.

    VI

Not to be realized because not to
Be seen, not to be loved nor hated because
Not to be realized. Weather by Franz Hals,

Brushed up by brushy winds in brushy clouds,
Wetted by blue, colder for white. Not to
Be spoken to, without a roof, without

First fruits, without the virginal of birds,
The dark-blown ceinture loosened, not relinquished.
Gay is, gay was, the gay forsythia

And yellow, yellow thins the Northern blue.
Without a name and nothing to be desired,
If only imagined but imagined well.

My house has changed a little in the sun.
The fragrance of the magnolias comes close,
False flick, false form, but falseness close to kin.

It must be visible or invisible,
Invisible or visible or both:
A seeing and unseeing in the eye.

The weather and the giant of the weather,
Say the weather, the mere weather, the mere air:
An abstraction blooded, as a man by thought.

VII

It feels good as it is without the giant,
A thinker of the first idea. Perhaps
The truth depends on a walk around a lake,

A composing as the body tires, a stop
To see hepatica, a stop to watch
A definition growing certain and

A wait within that certainty, a rest
In the swags of pine-trees bordering the lake.
Perhaps there are times of inherent excellence,

As when the cock crows on the left and all
Is well, incalculable balances,
At which a kind of Swiss perfection comes

And a familiar music of the machine
Sets up its Schwärmerei, not balances
That we achieve but balances that happen,

As a man and woman meet and love forthwith.
Perhaps there are moments of awakening,
Extreme, fortuitous, personal, in which

We more than awaken, sit on the edge of sleep,
As on an elevation, and behold
The academies like structures in a mist.

VIII

Can we compose a castle-fortress-home,
Even with the help of Viollet-le-Duc,
And set the MacCullough there as major man?

The first idea is an imagined thing
The pensive giant prone in violet space
May be the MacCullough, an expedient,

Logos and logic, crystal hypothesis,
Incipit and a form to speak the word
And every latent double in the word,

Beau linguist. But the MacCullough is MacCullough.
It does not follow that major man is man.
If MacCullough himself lay lounging by the sea,

Drowned in its washes, reading in the sound,
About the thinker of the first idea,
He might take habit, whether from wave or phrase,

Or power of the wave, or deepened speech,
Or a leaner being, moving in on him,
Of greater aptitude and apprehension,

As if the waves at last were never broken,
As if the language suddenly, with ease,
Said things it had laboriously spoken.

IX

The romantic intoning, the declaimed clairvoyance
Are parts of apotheosis, appropriate
And of its nature, the idiom thereof.

They differ from reason's click-clack, its applied
Enflashings. But apotheosis is not
The origin of the major man. He comes,

Compact in invincible foils, from reason,
Lighted at midnight by the studious eye,
Swaddled in revery, the object of

The hum of thoughts evaded in the mind,
Hidden from other thoughts, he that reposes
On a breast forever precious for that touch,

For whom the good of April falls tenderly,
Falls down, the cock-birds calling at the time.
My dame, sing for this person accurate songs.

He is and may be but oh! he is, he is,
This foundling of the infected past, so bright,
So moving in the manner of his hand.

Yet look not at his colored eyes. Give him
No names. Dismiss him from your images.
The hot of him is purest in the heart.

     x

The major abstraction is the idea of man
And major man is its exponent, abler
In the abstract than in his singular,

More fecund as principle than particle,
Happy fecundity, flor-abundant force,
In being more than an exception, part,

Though an heroic part, of the commonal.
The major abstraction is the commonal,
The inanimate, difficult visage. Who is it?

What rabbi, grown furious with human wish,
What chieftain, walking by himself, crying
Most miserable, most victorious,

Does not see these separate figures one by one,
And yet see only one, in his old coat,
His slouching pantaloons, beyond the town,

Looking for what was, where it used to be?
Cloudless the morning. It is he. The man
In that old coat, those sagging pantaloons,

It is of him, ephebe, to make, to confect
The final elegance, not to console
Nor sanctify, but plainly to propound.

IT MUST CHANGE

I

The old seraph, parcel-gilded, among violets
Inhaled the appointed odor, while the doves
Rose up like phantoms from chronologies.

The Italian girls wore jonquils in their hair
And these the seraph saw, had seen long since,
In the bandeaux of the mothers, would see again.

The bees came booming as if they had never gone,
As if hyacinths had never gone. We say
This changes and that changes. Thus the constant

Violets, doves, girls, bees and hyacinths
Are inconstant objects of inconstant cause
In a universe of inconstancy. This means

Night-blue is an inconstant thing. The seraph
Is satyr in Saturn, according to his thoughts.
It means the distaste we feel for this withered scene

Is that it has not changed enough. It remains,
It is a repetition. The bees come booming
As if— The pigeons clatter in the air.

An erotic perfume, half of the body, half
Of an obvious acid is sure what it intends
And the booming is blunt, not broken in subtleties.

II

The President ordains the bee to be
Immortal. The President ordains. But does
The body lift its heavy wing, take up,

Again, an inexhaustible being, rise
Over the loftiest antagonist
To drone the green phrases of its juvenal?

Why should the bee recapture a lost blague,
Find a deep echo in a horn and buzz
The bottomless trophy, new hornsman after old?

The President has apples on the table
And barefoot servants round him, who adjust
The curtains to a metaphysical t

And the banners of the nation flutter, burst
On the flag-poles in a red-blue dazzle, whack
At the halyards. Why, then, when in golden fury

Spring vanishes the scraps of winter, why
Should there be a question of returning or
Of death in memory's dream? Is spring a sleep?

This warmth is for lovers at last accomplishing
Their love, this beginning, not resuming, this
Booming and booming of the new-come bee.

III

The great statue of the General Du Puy
Rested immobile, though neighboring catafalques
Bore off the residents of its noble Place.

The right, uplifted foreleg of the horse
Suggested that, at the final funeral,
The music halted and the horse stood still.

On Sundays, lawyers in their promenades
Approached this strongly-heightened effigy
To study the past, and doctors, having bathed

Themselves with care, sought out the nerveless frame
Of a suspension, a permanence, so rigid
That it made the General a bit absurd,

Changed his true flesh to an inhuman bronze.
There never had been, never could be, such
A man. The lawyers disbelieved, the doctors

Said that as keen, illustrious ornament,
As a setting for geraniums, the General,
The very Place Du Puy, in fact, belonged

Among our more vestigial states of mind.
Nothing had happened because nothing had changed.
Yet the General was rubbish in the end.

IV

Two things of opposite natures seem to depend
On one another, as a man depends
On a woman, day on night, the imagined

On the real. This is the origin of change.
Winter and spring, cold copulars, embrace
And forth the particulars of rapture come.

Music falls on the silence like a sense,
A passion that we feel, not understand.
Morning and afternoon are clasped together

And North and South are an intrinsic couple
And sun and rain a plural, like two lovers
That walk away as one in the greenest body.

In solitude the trumpets of solitude
Are not of another solitude resounding;
A little string speaks for a crowd of voices.

The partaker partakes of that which changes him.
The child that touches takes character from the thing,
The body, it touches. The captain and his men

Are one and the sailor and the sea are one.
Follow after, O my companion, my fellow, my self,
Sister and solace, brother and delight.

v

On a blue island in a sky-wide water
The wild orange trees continued to bloom and to bear,
Long after the planter's death. A few limes remained,

Where his house had fallen, three scraggy trees weighted
With garbled green. These were the planter's turquoise
And his orange blotches, these were his zero green,

A green baked greener in the greenest sun.
These were his beaches, his sea-myrtles in
White sand, his patter of the long sea-slushes.

There was an island beyond him on which rested,
An island to the South, on which rested like
A mountain, a pineapple pungent as Cuban summer.

And là-bas, là-bas, the cool bananas grew,
Hung heavily on the great banana tree,
Which pierces clouds and bends on half the world.

He thought often of the land from which he came,
How that whole country was a melon, pink
If seen rightly and yet a possible red.

An unaffected man in a negative light
Could not have borne his labor nor have died
Sighing that he should leave the banjo's twang.

VI

Bethou me, said sparrow, to the crackled blade,
And you, and you, bethou me as you blow,
When in my coppice you behold me be.

Ah, ké! the bloody wren, the felon jay,
Ké-ké, the jug-throated robin pouring out,
Bethou, bethou, bethou me in my glade.

There was such idiot minstrelsy in rain,
So many clappers going without bells,
That these bethous compose a heavenly gong.

One voice repeating, one tireless chorister,
The phrases of a single phrase, ké-ké,
A single text, granite monotony,

One sole face, like a photograph of fate,
Glass-blower's destiny, bloodless episcopus,
Eye without lid, mind without any dream—

These are of minstrels lacking minstrelsy,
Of an earth in which the first leaf is the tale
Of leaves, in which the sparrow is a bird

Of stone, that never changes. Bethou him, you
And you, bethou him and bethou. It is
A sound like any other. It will end.

After a lustre of the moon, we say
We have not the need of any paradise,
We have not the need of any seducing hymn.

It is true. Tonight the lilacs magnify
The easy passion, the ever-ready love
Of the lover that lies within us and we breathe

An odor evoking nothing, absolute.
We encounter in the dead middle of the night
The purple odor, the abundant bloom.

The lover sighs as for accessible bliss,
Which he can take within him on his breath,
Possess in his heart, conceal and nothing known.

For easy passion and ever-ready love
Are of our earthy birth and here and now
And where we live and everywhere we live,

As in the top-cloud of a May night-evening,
As in the courage of the ignorant man,
Who chants by book, in the heat of the scholar, who writes

The book, hot for another accessible bliss:
The fluctuations of certainty, the change
Of degrees of perception in the scholar's dark.

VIII

On her trip around the world, Nanzia Nunzio
Confronted Ozymandias. She went
Alone and like a vestal long-prepared.

I am the spouse. She took her necklace off
And laid it in the sand. As I am, I am
The spouse. She opened her stone-studded belt.

I am the spouse, divested of bright gold,
The spouse beyond emerald or amethyst,
Beyond the burning body that I bear.

I am the woman stripped more nakedly
Than nakedness, standing before an inflexible
Order, saying I am the contemplated spouse.

Speak to me that, which spoken, will array me
In its own only precious ornament.
Set on me the spirit's diamond coronal.

Clothe me entire in the final filament,
So that I tremble with such love so known
And myself am precious for your perfecting.

Then Ozymandias said the spouse, the bride
Is never naked. A fictive covering
Weaves always glistening from the heart and mind.

IX

The poem goes from the poet's gibberish to
The gibberish of the vulgate and back again.
Does it move to and fro or is it of both

At once? Is it a luminous flittering
Or the concentration of a cloudy day?
Is there a poem that never reaches words

And one that chaffers the time away?
Is the poem both peculiar and general?
There's a meditation there, in which there seems

To be an evasion, a thing not apprehended or
Not apprehended well. Does the poet
Evade us, as in a senseless element?

Evade, this hot, dependent orator,
The spokesman at our bluntest barriers,
Exponent by a form of speech, the speaker

Of a speech only a little of the tongue?
It is the gibberish of the vulgate that he seeks.
He tries by a peculiar speech to speak

The peculiar potency of the general,
To compound the imagination's Latin with
The lingua franca et jocundissima.

                    x

A bench was his catalepsy, Theatre
Of Trope. He sat in the park. The water of
The lake was full of artificial things,

Like a page of music, like an upper air,
Like a momentary color, in which swans
Were seraphs, were saints, were changing essences.

The west wind was the music, the motion, the force
To which the swans curveted, a will to change,
A will to make iris frettings on the blank.

There was a will to change, a necessitous
And present way, a presentation, a kind
Of volatile world, too constant to be denied,

The eye of a vagabond in metaphor
That catches our own. The casual is not
Enough. The freshness of transformation is

The freshness of a world. It is our own,
It is ourselves, the freshness of ourselves,
And that necessity and that presentation

Are rubbings of a glass in which we peer.
Of these beginnings, gay and green, propose
The suitable amours. Time will write them down.

IT MUST GIVE PLEASURE

I

To sing jubilas at exact, accustomed times,
To be crested and wear the mane of a multitude
And so, as part, to exult with its great throat,

To speak of joy and to sing of it, borne on
The shoulders of joyous men, to feel the heart
That is the common, the bravest fundament,

This is a facile exercise. Jerome
Begat the tubas and the fire-wind strings,
The golden fingers picking dark-blue air:

For companies of voices moving there,
To find of sound the bleakest ancestor,
To find of light a music issuing

Whereon it falls in more than sensual mode.
But the difficultest rigor is forthwith,
On the image of what we see, to catch from that

Irrational moment its unreasoning,
As when the sun comes rising, when the sea
Clears deeply, when the moon hangs on the wall

Of heaven-haven. These are not things transformed.
Yet we are shaken by them as if they were.
We reason about them with a later reason.

          II

The blue woman, linked and lacquered, at her window
Did not desire that feathery argentines
Should be cold silver, neither that frothy clouds

Should foam, be foamy waves, should move like them,
Nor that the sexual blossoms should repose
Without their fierce addictions, nor that the heat

Of summer, growing fragrant in the night,
Should strengthen her abortive dreams and take
In sleep its natural form. It was enough

For her that she remembered: the argentines
Of spring come to their places in the grape leaves
To cool their ruddy pulses; the frothy clouds

Are nothing but frothy clouds; the frothy blooms
Waste without puberty; and afterward,
When the harmonious heat of August pines

Enters the room, it drowses and is the night.
It was enough for her that she remembered.
The blue woman looked and from her window named

The corals of the dogwood, cold and clear,
Cold, coldly delineating, being real,
Clear and, except for the eye, without intrusion.

III

A lasting visage in a lasting bush,
A face of stone in an unending red,
Red-emerald, red-slitted-blue, a face of slate,

An ancient forehead hung with heavy hair,
The channel slots of rain, the red-rose-red
And weathered and the ruby-water-worn,

The vines around the throat, the shapeless lips,
The frown like serpents basking on the brow,
The spent feeling leaving nothing of itself,

Red-in-red repetitions never going
Away, a little rusty, a little rouged,
A little roughened and ruder, a crown

The eye could not escape, a red renown
Blowing itself upon the tedious ear.
An effulgence faded, dull cornelian

Too venerably used. That might have been.
It might and might have been. But as it was,
A dead shepherd brought tremendous chords from hell

And bade the sheep carouse. Or so they said.
Children in love with them brought early flowers
And scattered them about, no two alike.

IV

We reason of these things with later reason
And we make of what we see, what we see clearly
And have seen, a place dependent on ourselves.

There was a mystic marriage in Catawba,
At noon it was on the mid-day of the year
Between a great captain and the maiden Bawda.

This was their ceremonial hymn: Anon
We loved but would no marriage make. Anon
The one refused the other one to take,

Foreswore the sipping of the marriage wine.
Each must the other take not for his high,
His puissant front nor for her subtle sound,

The shoo-shoo-shoo of secret cymbals round.
Each must the other take as sign, short sign
To stop the whirlwind, balk the elements.

The great captain loved the ever-hill Catawba
And therefore married Bawda, whom he found there,
And Bawda loved the captain as she loved the sun.

They married well because the marriage-place
Was what they loved. It was neither heaven nor hell.
They were love's characters come face to face.

V

We drank Meursault, ate lobster Bombay with mango
Chutney. Then the Canon Aspirin declaimed
Of his sister, in what a sensible ecstasy

She lived in her house. She had two daughters, one
Of four, and one of seven, whom she dressed
The way a painter of pauvred color paints.

But still she painted them, appropriate to
Their poverty, a gray-blue yellowed out
With ribbon, a rigid statement of them, white,

With Sunday pearls, her widow's gayety.
She hid them under simple names. She held
Them closelier to her by rejecting dreams.

The words they spoke were voices that she heard.
She looked at them and saw them as they were
And what she felt fought off the barest phrase.

The Canon Aspirin, having said these things,
Reflected, humming an outline of a fugue
Of praise, a conjugation done by choirs.

Yet when her children slept, his sister herself
Demanded of sleep, in the excitements of silence
Only the unmuddled self of sleep, for them.

VI

When at long midnight the Canon came to sleep
And normal things had yawned themselves away,
The nothingness was a nakedness, a point,

Beyond which fact could not progress as fact.
Thereon the learning of the man conceived
Once more night's pale illuminations, gold

Beneath, far underneath, the surface of
His eye and audible in the mountain of
His ear, the very material of his mind.

So that he was the ascending wings he saw
And moved on them in orbits' outer stars
Descending to the children's bed, on which

They lay. Forth then with huge pathetic force
Straight to the utmost crown of night he flew.
The nothingness was a nakedness, a point

Beyond which thought could not progress as thought.
He had to choose. But it was not a choice
Between excluding things. It was not a choice

Between, but of. He chose to include the things
That in each other are included, the whole,
The complicate, the amassing harmony.

VII

He imposes orders as he thinks of them,
As the fox and snake do. It is a brave affair.
Next he builds capitols and in their corridors,

Whiter than wax, sonorous, fame as it is,
He establishes statues of reasonable men,
Who surpassed the most literate owl, the most erudite

Of elephants. But to impose is not
To discover. To discover an order as of
A season, to discover summer and know it,

To discover winter and know it well, to find,
Not to impose, not to have reasoned at all,
Out of nothing to have come on major weather,

It is possible, possible, possible. It must
Be possible. It must be that in time
The real will from its crude compoundings come,

Seeming, at first, a beast disgorged, unlike,
Warmed by a desperate milk. To find the real,
To be stripped of every fiction except one,

The fiction of an absolute— Angel,
Be silent in your luminous cloud and hear
The luminous melody of proper sound.

VIII

What am I to believe? If the angel in his cloud,
Serenely gazing at the violet abyss,
Plucks on his strings to pluck abysmal glory,

Leaps downward through evening's revelations, and
On his spredden wings, needs nothing but deep space,
Forgets the gold center, the golden destiny,

Grows warm in the motionless motion of his flight,
Am I that imagine this angel less satisfied?
Are the wings his, the lapis-haunted air?

Is it he or is it I that experience this?
Is it I then that keep saying there is an hour
Filled with expressible bliss, in which I have

No need, am happy, forget need's golden hand,
Am satisfied without solacing majesty,
And if there is an hour there is a day,

There is a month, a year, there is a time
In which majesty is a mirror of the self:
I have not but I am and as I am, I am.

These external regions, what do we fill them with
Except reflections, the escapades of death,
Cinderella fulfilling herself beneath the roof?

IX

Whistle aloud, too weedy wren. I can
Do all that angels can. I enjoy like them,
Like men besides, like men in light secluded,

Enjoying angels. Whistle, forced bugler,
That bugles for the mate, nearby the nest,
Cock bugler, whistle and bugle and stop just short,

Red robin, stop in your preludes, practicing
Mere repetitions. These things at least comprise
An occupation, an exercise, a work,

A thing final in itself and, therefore, good:
One of the vast repetitions final in
Themselves and, therefore, good, the going round

And round and round, the merely going round,
Until merely going round is a final good,
The way wine comes at a table in a wood.

And we enjoy like men, the way a leaf
Above the table spins its constant spin,
So that we look at it with pleasure, look

At it spinning its eccentric measure. Perhaps,
The man-hero is not the exceptional monster,
But he that of repetition is most master.

X

Fat girl, terrestrial, my summer, my night,
How is it I find you in difference, see you there
In a moving contour, a change not quite completed?

You are familiar yet an aberration.
Civil, madam, I am, but underneath
A tree, this unprovoked sensation requires

That I should name you flatly, waste no words,
Check your evasions, hold you to yourself.
Even so when I think of you as strong or tired,

Bent over work, anxious, content, alone,
You remain the more than natural figure. You
Become the soft-footed phantom, the irrational

Distortion, however fragrant, however dear.
That's it: the more than rational distortion,
The fiction that results from feeling. Yes, that.

They will get it straight one day at the Sorbonne.
We shall return at twilight from the lecture
Pleased that the irrational is rational,

Until flicked by feeling, in a gildered street,
I call you by name, my green, my fluent mundo.
You will have stopped revolving except in crystal.

Soldier, there is a war between the mind
And sky, between thought and day and night. It is
For that the poet is always in the sun,

Patches the moon together in his room
To his Virgilian cadences, up down,
Up down. It is a war that never ends.

Yet it depends on yours. The two are one.
They are a plural, a right and left, a pair,
Two parallels that meet if only in

The meeting of their shadows or that meet
In a book in a barrack, a letter from Malay.
But your war ends. And after it you return

With six meats and twelve wines or else without
To walk another room . . . Monsieur and comrade,
The soldier is poor without the poet's lines,

His petty syllabi, the sounds that stick,
Inevitably modulating, in the blood.
And war for war, each has its gallant kind.

How simply the fictive hero becomes the real;
How gladly with proper words the soldier dies,
If he must, or lives on the bread of faithful speech.

THE AURORAS OF AUTUMN

I

This is where the serpent lives, the bodiless.
His head is air. Beneath his tip at night
Eyes open and fix on us in every sky.

Or is this another wriggling out of the egg,
Another image at the end of the cave,
Another bodiless for the body's slough?

This is where the serpent lives. This is his nest,
These fields, these hills, these tinted distances,
And the pines above and along and beside the sea.

This is form gulping after formlessness,
Skin flashing to wished-for disappearances
And the serpent body flashing without the skin.

This is the height emerging and its base . . .
These lights may finally attain a pole
In the midmost midnight and find the serpent there,

In another nest, the master of the maze
Of body and air and forms and images,
Relentlessly in possession of happiness.

This is his poison: that we should disbelieve
Even that. His meditations in the ferns,
When he moved so slightly to make sure of sun,

Made us no less as sure. We saw in his head,
Black beaded on the rock, the flecked animal,
The moving grass, the Indian in his glade.

Farewell to an idea . . . A cabin stands,
Deserted, on a beach. It is white,
As by a custom or according to

An ancestral theme or as a consequence
Of an infinite course. The flowers against the wall
Are white, a little dried, a kind of mark

Reminding, trying to remind, of a white
That was different, something else, last year
Or before, not the white of an aging afternoon,

Whether fresher or duller, whether of winter cloud
Or of winter sky, from horizon to horizon.
The wind is blowing the sand across the floor.

Here, being visible is being white,
Is being of the solid of white, the accomplishment
Of an extremist in an exercise . . .

The season changes. A cold wind chills the beach.
The long lines of it grow longer, emptier,
A darkness gathers though it does not fall

And the whiteness grows less vivid on the wall.
The man who is walking turns blankly on the sand.
He observes how the north is always enlarging the change,

With its frigid brilliances, its blue-red sweeps
And gusts of great enkindlings, its polar green,
The color of ice and fire and solitude.

III

Farewell to an idea . . . The mother's face,
The purpose of the poem, fills the room.
They are together, here, and it is warm,

With none of the prescience of oncoming dreams.
It is evening. The house is evening, half dissolved.
Only the half they can never possess remains,

Still-starred. It is the mother they possess,
Who gives transparence to their present peace.
She makes that gentler that can gentle be.

And yet she too is dissolved, she is destroyed.
She gives transparence. But she has grown old.
The necklace is a carving not a kiss.

The soft hands are a motion not a touch.
The house will crumble and the books will burn.
They are at ease in a shelter of the mind

And the house is of the mind and they and time,
Together, all together. Boreal night
Will look like frost as it approaches them

And to the mother as she falls asleep
And as they say good-night, good-night. Upstairs
The windows will be lighted, not the rooms.

A wind will spread its windy grandeurs round
And knock like a rifle-butt against the door.
The wind will command them with invincible sound.

IV

Farewell to an idea . . . The cancellings,
The negations are never final. The father sits
In space, wherever he sits, of bleak regard,

As one that is strong in the bushes of his eyes.
He says no to no and yes to yes. He says yes
To no; and in saying yes he says farewell.

He measures the velocities of change.
He leaps from heaven to heaven more rapidly
Than bad angels leap from heaven to hell in flames.

But now he sits in quiet and green-a-day.
He assumes the great speeds of space and flutters them
From cloud to cloudless, cloudless to keen clear

In flights of eye and ear, the highest eye
And the lowest ear, the deep ear that discerns,
At evening, things that attend it until it hears

The supernatural preludes of its own,
At the moment when the angelic eye defines
Its actors approaching, in company, in their masks.

Master O master seated by the fire
And yet in space and motionless and yet
Of motion the ever-brightening origin,

Profound, and yet the king and yet the crown,
Look at this present throne. What company,
In masks, can choir it with the naked wind?

V

The mother invites humanity to her house
And table. The father fetches tellers of tales
And musicians who mute much, muse much, on the tales.

The father fetches negresses to dance,
Among the children, like curious ripenesses
Of pattern in the dance's ripening.

For these the musicians make insidious tones,
Clawing the sing-song of their instruments.
The children laugh and jangle a tinny time.

The father fetches pageants out of air,
Scenes of the theatre, vistas and blocks of woods
And curtains like a naive pretence of sleep.

Among these the musicians strike the instinctive poem.
The father fetches his unherded herds,
Of barbarous tongue, slavered and panting halves

Of breath, obedient to his trumpet's touch.
This then is Chatillon or as you please.
We stand in the tumult of a festival.

What festival? This loud, disordered mooch?
These hospitaliers? These brute-like guests?
These musicians dubbing at a tragedy,

A-dub, a-dub, which is made up of this:
That there are no lines to speak? There is no play.
Or, the persons act one merely by being here.

VI

It is a theatre floating through the clouds,
Itself a cloud, although of misted rock
And mountains running like water, wave on wave,

Through waves of light. It is of cloud transformed
To cloud transformed again, idly, the way
A season changes color to no end,

Except the lavishing of itself in change,
As light changes yellow into gold and gold
To its opal elements and fire's delight,

Splashed wide-wise because it likes magnificence
And the solemn pleasures of magnificent space.
The cloud drifts idly through half-thought-of forms.

The theatre is filled with flying birds,
Wild wedges, as of a volcano's smoke, palm-eyed
And vanishing, a web in a corridor

Or massive portico. A capitol,
It may be, is emerging or has just
Collapsed. The denouement has to be postponed . . .

This is nothing until in a single man contained,
Nothing until this named thing nameless is
And is destroyed. He opens the door of his house

On flames. The scholar of one candle sees
An Arctic effulgence flaring on the frame
Of everything he is. And he feels afraid.

VII

Is there an imagination that sits enthroned
As grim as it is benevolent, the just
And the unjust, which in the midst of summer stops

To imagine winter? When the leaves are dead,
Does it take its place in the north and enfold itself,
Goat-leaper, crystalled and luminous, sitting

In highest night? And do these heavens adorn
And proclaim it, the white creator of black, jetted
By extinguishings, even of planets as may be,

Even of earth, even of sight, in snow,
Except as needed by way of majesty,
In the sky, as crown and diamond cabala?

It leaps through us, through all our heavens leaps,
Extinguishing our planets, one by one,
Leaving, of where we were and looked, of where

We knew each other and of each other thought,
A shivering residue, chilled and foregone,
Except for that crown and mystical cabala.

But it dare not leap by chance in its own dark.
It must change from destiny to slight caprice.
And thus its jetted tragedy, its stele

And shape and mournful making move to find
What must unmake it and, at last, what can,
Say, a flippant communication under the moon.

VIII

There may be always a time of innocence.
There is never a place. Or if there is no time,
If it is not a thing of time, nor of place,

Existing in the idea of it, alone,
In the sense against calamity, it is not
Less real. For the oldest and coldest philosopher,

There is or may be a time of innocence
As pure principle. Its nature is its end,
That it should be, and yet not be, a thing

That pinches the pity of the pitiful man,
Like a book at evening beautiful but untrue,
Like a book on rising beautiful and true.

It is like a thing of ether that exists
Almost as predicate. But it exists,
It exists, it is visible, it is, it is.

So, then, these lights are not a spell of light,
A saying out of a cloud, but innocence.
An innocence of the earth and no false sign

Or symbol of malice. That we partake thereof,
Lie down like children in this holiness,
As if, awake, we lay in the quiet of sleep,

As if the innocent mother sang in the dark
Of the room and on an accordion, half-heard,
Created the time and place in which we breathed . . .

IX

And of each other thought—in the idiom
Of the work, in the idiom of an innocent earth,
Not of the enigma of the guilty dream.

We were as Danes in Denmark all day long
And knew each other well, hale-hearted landsmen,
For whom the outlandish was another day

Of the week, queerer than Sunday. We thought alike
And that made brothers of us in a home
In which we fed on being brothers, fed

And fattened as on a decorous honeycomb.
This drama that we live— We lay sticky with sleep.
This sense of the activity of fate—

The rendezvous, when she came alone,
By her coming became a freedom of the two,
An isolation which only the two could share.

Shall we be found hanging in the trees next spring?
Of what disaster is this the imminence:
Bare limbs, bare trees and a wind as sharp as salt?

The stars are putting on their glittering belts.
They throw around their shoulders cloaks that flash
Like a great shadow's last embellishment.

It may come tomorrow in the simplest word,
Almost as part of innocence, almost,
Almost as the tenderest and the truest part.

X

An unhappy people in a happy world—
Read, rabbi, the phases of this difference.
An unhappy people in an unhappy world—

Here are too many mirrors for misery.
A happy people in an unhappy world—
It cannot be. There's nothing there to roll

On the expressive tongue, the finding fang.
A happy people in a happy world—
Buffo! A ball, an opera, a bar.

Turn back to where we were when we began:
An unhappy people in a happy world.
Now, solemnize the secretive syllables.

Read to the congregation, for today
And for tomorrow, this extremity,
This contrivance of the spectre of the spheres,

Contriving balance to contrive a whole,
The vital, the never-failing genius,
Fulfilling his meditations, great and small.

In these unhappy he meditates a whole,
The full of fortune and the full of fate,
As if he lived all lives, that he might know,

In hall harridan, not hushful paradise,
To a haggling of wind and weather, by these lights
Like a blaze of summer straw, in winter's nick.

In the hard brightness of that winter day
The sea was frozen solid and Hans heard,
By his drift-fire, on the shore, the difference
Between loud water and loud wind, between that
Which has no accurate syllables and that
Which cries *so blau* and cries again *so lind*
Und so lau, between sound without meaning and speech,
Of clay and wattles made as it ascends
And *hear it* as it falls *in the deep heart's core.*
A steamer lay near him, foundered in the ice.

So blau, so blau . . . Hans listened by the fire.
New stars that were a foot across came out
And shone. *And a small cabin build there.*
So lind. The wind blazed as they sang. *So lau.*
The great ship, Balayne, lay frozen in the sea.
The one-foot stars were couriers of its death
To the wild limits of its habitation.
These were not tepid stars of torpid places
But bravest at midnight and in lonely spaces,
They looked back at Hans' look with savage faces.

The wet weed sputtered, the fire died down, the cold
Was like a sleep. The sea was a sea he dreamed.
Yet Hans lay wide awake. *And live alone*
In the bee-loud glade. Lights on the steamer moved.
Men would be starting at dawn to walk ashore.
They would be afraid of the sun: what it might be,
Afraid of the country angels of those skies,
The finned flutterings and gaspings of the ice,
As if whatever in water strove to speak
Broke dialect in a break of memory.

The sun might rise and it might not and if
It rose, ashen and red and yellow, each
Opaque, in orange circlet, nearer than it
Had ever been before, no longer known,
No more that which most of all brings back the known,
But that which destroys it completely by this light
For that, or a motion not in the astronomies,
Beyond the habit of sense, anarchic shape
Afire—it might and it might not in that
Gothic blue, speed home its portents to their ends.

It might become a wheel spoked red and white
In alternate stripes converging at a point
Of flame on the line, with a second wheel below,
Just rising, accompanying, arranged to cross,
Through weltering illuminations, humps
Of billows, downward, toward the drift-fire shore.
It might come bearing, out of chaos, kin
Smeared, smoked, and drunken of thin potencies,
Lashing at images in the atmosphere,
Ringed round and barred, with eyes held in their hands,

And capable of incapably evil thought:
Slight gestures that could rend the palpable ice,
Or melt Arcturus to ingots dropping drops,
Or spill night out in brilliant vanishings,
Whirlpools of darkness in whirlwinds of light . . .
The miff-maff-muff of water, the vocables
Of the wind, the glassily-sparkling particles
Of the mind— They would soon climb down the side of the ship.
They would march single file, with electric lamps, alert
For a tidal undulation underneath.

LARGE RED MAN READING

There were ghosts that returned to earth to hear his phrases,
As he sat there reading, aloud, the great blue tabulae.
They were those from the wilderness of stars that had expected more.

There were those that returned to hear him read from the poem of life,
Of the pans above the stove, the pots on the table, the tulips among them.
They were those that would have wept to step barefoot into reality,

That would have wept and been happy, have shivered in the frost
And cried out to feel it again, have run fingers over leaves
And against the most coiled thorn, have seized on what was ugly

And laughed, as he sat there reading, from out of the purple tabulae,
The outlines of being and its expressings, the syllables of its law:
Poesis, poesis, the literal characters, the vatic lines,

Which in those ears and in those thin, those spended hearts,
Took on color, took on shape and the size of things as they are
And spoke the feeling for them, which was what they had lacked.

THIS SOLITUDE OF CATARACTS

He never felt twice the same about the flecked river,
Which kept flowing and never the same way twice, flowing

Through many places, as if it stood still in one,
Fixed like a lake on which the wild ducks fluttered,

Ruffling its common reflections, thought-like Monadnocks.
There seemed to be an apostrophe that was not spoken.

There was so much that was real that was not real at all.
He wanted to feel the same way over and over.

He wanted the river to go on flowing the same way,
To keep on flowing. He wanted to walk beside it,

Under the buttonwoods, beneath a moon nailed fast.
He wanted his heart to stop beating and his mind to rest

In a permanent realization, without any wild ducks
Or mountains that were not mountains, just to know how it would be,

Just to know how it would feel, released from destruction,
To be a bronze man breathing under archaic lapis,

Without the oscillations of planetary pass-pass,
Breathing his bronzen breath at the azury center of time.

THE BEGINNING

So summer comes in the end to these few stains
And the rust and rot of the door through which she went.

The house is empty. But here is where she sat
To comb her dewy hair, a touchless light,

Perplexed by its darker iridescences.
This was the glass in which she used to look

At the moment's being, without history,
The self of summer perfectly perceived,

And feel its country gaiety and smile
And be surprised and tremble, hand and lip.

This is the chair from which she gathered up
Her dress, the carefulest, commodious weave

Inwoven by a weaver to twelve bells . . .
The dress is lying, cast-off, on the floor.

Now, the first tutoyers of tragedy
Speak softly, to begin with, in the eaves.

THE COUNTRYMAN

Swatara, Swatara, black river,
Descending, out of the cap of midnight,
Toward the cape at which
You enter the swarthy sea,

Swatara, Swatara, heavy the hills
Are, hanging above you, as you move,
Move blackly and without crystal.
A countryman walks beside you.

He broods of neither cap nor cape,
But only of your swarthy motion,
But always of the swarthy water,
Of which Swatara is the breathing,

The name. He does not speak beside you.
He is there because he wants to be
And because being there in the heavy hills
And along the moving of the water—

Being there is being in a place,
As of a character everywhere,
The place of a swarthy presence moving,
Slowly, to the look of a swarthy name.

THE ULTIMATE POEM IS ABSTRACT

This day writhes with what? The lecturer
On This Beautiful World Of Ours composes himself
And hems the planet rose and haws it ripe,

And red, and right. The particular question—here
The particular answer to the particular question
Is not in point—the question is in point.

If the day writhes, it is not with revelations.
One goes on asking questions. That, then, is one
Of the categories. So said, this placid space

Is changed. It is not so blue as we thought. To be blue,
There must be no questions. It is an intellect
Of windings round and dodges to and fro,

Writhings in wrong obliques and distances,
Not an intellect in which we are fleet: present
Everywhere in space at once, cloud-pole

Of communication. It would be enough
If we were ever, just once, at the middle, fixed
In This Beautiful World Of Ours and not as now,

Helplessly at the edge, enough to be
Complete, because at the middle, if only in sense,
And in that enormous sense, merely enjoy.

BOUQUET OF ROSES IN SUNLIGHT

Say that it is a crude effect, black reds,
Pink yellows, orange whites, too much as they are
To be anything else in the sunlight of the room,

Too much as they are to be changed by metaphor,
Too actual, things that in being real
Make any imaginings of them lesser things.

And yet this effect is a consequence of the way
We feel and, therefore, is not real, except
In our sense of it, our sense of the fertilest red,

Of yellow as first color and of white,
In which the sense lies still, as a man lies,
Enormous, in a completing of his truth.

Our sense of these things changes and they change,
Not as in metaphor, but in our sense
Of them. So sense exceeds all metaphor.

It exceeds the heavy changes of the light.
It is like a flow of meanings with no speech
And of as many meanings as of men.

We are two that use these roses as we are,
In seeing them. This is what makes them seem
So far beyond the rhetorician's touch.

A PRIMITIVE LIKE AN ORB

I

The essential poem at the center of things,
The arias that spiritual fiddlings make,
Have gorged the cast-iron of our lives with good
And the cast-iron of our works. But it is, dear sirs,
A difficult apperception, this gorging good,
Fetched by such slick-eyed nymphs, this essential gold,
This fortune's finding, disposed and re-disposed
By such slight genii in such pale air.

II

We do not prove the existence of the poem.
It is something seen and known in lesser poems.
It is the huge, high harmony that sounds
A little and a little, suddenly,
By means of a separate sense. It is and it
Is not and, therefore, is. In the instant of speech,
The breadth of an accelerando moves,
Captives the being, widens—and was there.

III

What milk there is in such captivity,
What wheaten bread and oaten cake and kind,
Green guests and table in the woods and songs
At heart, within an instant's motion, within
A space grown wide, the inevitable blue
Of secluded thunder, an illusion, as it was,
Oh as, always too heavy for the sense
To seize, the obscurest as, the distant was . . .

IV

One poem proves another and the whole,
For the clairvoyant men that need no proof:
The lover, the believer and the poet.
Their words are chosen out of their desire,
The joy of language, when it is themselves.
With these they celebrate the central poem,
The fulfillment of fulfillments, in opulent,
Last terms, the largest, bulging still with more,

V

Until the used-to earth and sky, and the tree
And cloud, the used-to tree and used-to cloud,
Lose the old uses that they made of them,
And they: these men, and earth and sky, inform
Each other by sharp informations, sharp,
Free knowledges, secreted until then,
Breaches of that which held them fast. It is
As if the central poem became the world,

VI

And the world the central poem, each one the mate
Of the other, as if summer was a spouse,
Espoused each morning, each long afternoon,
And the mate of summer: her mirror and her look,
Her only place and person, a self of her
That speaks, denouncing separate selves, both one.
The essential poem begets the others. The light
Of it is not a light apart, up-hill.

VII

The central poem is the poem of the whole,
The poem of the composition of the whole,
The composition of blue sea and of green,
Of blue light and of green, as lesser poems,
And the miraculous multiplex of lesser poems,
Not merely into a whole, but a poem of
The whole, the essential compact of the parts,
The roundness that pulls tight the final ring

VIII

And that which in an altitude would soar,
A vis, a principle or, it may be,
The meditation of a principle,
Or else an inherent order active to be
Itself, a nature to its natives all
Beneficence, a repose, utmost repose,
The muscles of a magnet aptly felt,
A giant, on the horizon, glistening,

IX

And in bright excellence adorned, crested
With every prodigal, familiar fire,
And unfamiliar escapades: whirroos
And scintillant sizzlings such as children like,
Vested in the serious folds of majesty,
Moving around and behind, a following,
A source of trumpeting seraphs in the eye,
A source of pleasant outbursts on the ear.

X

It is a giant, always, that is evolved,
To be in scale, unless virtue cuts him, snips
Both size and solitude or thinks it does,
As in a signed photograph on a mantelpiece.
But the virtuoso never leaves his shape,
Still on the horizon elongates his cuts,
And still angelic and still plenteous,
Imposes power by the power of his form.

XI

Here, then, is an abstraction given head,
A giant on the horizon, given arms,
A massive body and long legs, stretched out,
A definition with an illustration, not
Too exactly labelled, a large among the smalls
Of it, a close, parental magnitude,
At the center on the horizon, concentrum, grave
And prodigious person, patron of origins.

XII

That's it. The lover writes, the believer hears,
The poet mumbles and the painter sees,
Each one, his fated eccentricity,
As a part, but part, but tenacious particle,
Of the skeleton of the ether, the total
Of letters, prophecies, perceptions, clods
Of color, the giant of nothingness, each one
And the giant ever changing, living in change.

THE WOMAN IN SUNSHINE

It is only that this warmth and movement are like
The warmth and movement of a woman.

It is not that there is any image in the air
Nor the beginning nor end of a form:

It is empty. But a woman in threadless gold
Burns us with brushings of her dress

And a dissociated abundance of being,
More definite for what she is—

Because she is disembodied,
Bearing the odors of the summer fields,

Confessing the taciturn and yet indifferent,
Invisibly clear, the only love.

WORLD WITHOUT PECULIARITY

The day is great and strong—
But his father was strong, that lies now
In the poverty of dirt.

Nothing could be more hushed than the way
The moon moves toward the night.
But what his mother was returns and cries on his breast.

The red ripeness of round leaves is thick
With the spices of red summer.
But she that he loved turns cold at his light touch.

What good is it that the earth is justified,
That it is complete, that it is an end,
That in itself it is enough?

It is the earth itself that is humanity . . .
He is the inhuman son and she,
She is the fateful mother, whom he does not know.

She is the day, the walk of the moon
Among the breathless spices and, sometimes,
He, too, is human and difference disappears

And the poverty of dirt, the thing upon his breast,
The hating woman, the meaningless place,
Become a single being, sure and true.

PUELLA PARVULA

Every thread of summer is at last unwoven.
By one caterpillar is great Africa devoured
And Gibraltar is dissolved like spit in the wind.

But over the wind, over the legends of its roaring,
The elephant on the roof and its elephantine blaring,
The bloody lion in the yard at night or ready to spring

From the clouds in the midst of trembling trees
Making a great gnashing, over the water wallows
Of a vacant sea declaiming with wide throat,

Over all these the mighty imagination triumphs
Like a trumpet and says, in this season of memory,
When the leaves fall like things mournful of the past,

Keep quiet in the heart, O wild bitch. O mind
Gone wild, be what he tells you to be: *Puella.*
Write *pax* across the window pane. And then

Be still. The *summarium in excelsis* begins . . .
Flame, sound, fury composed . . . Hear what he says,
The dauntless master, as he starts the human tale.

WHAT WE SEE IS WHAT WE THINK

At twelve, the disintegration of afternoon
Began, the return to phantomerei, if not
To phantoms. Till then, it had been the other way:

One imagined the violet trees but the trees stood green,
At twelve, as green as ever they would be.
The sky was blue beyond the vaultiest phrase.

Twelve meant as much as: the end of normal time,
Straight up, an élan without harrowing,
The imprescriptible zenith, free of harangue,

Twelve and the first gray second after, a kind
Of violet gray, a green violet, a thread
To weave a shadow's leg or sleeve, a scrawl

On the pedestal, an ambitious page dog-eared
At the upper right, a pyramid with one side
Like a spectral cut in its perception, a tilt

And its tawny caricature and tawny life,
Another thought, the paramount ado . . .
Since what we think is never what we see.

QUESTIONS ARE REMARKS

In the weed of summer comes this green sprout why.
The sun aches and ails and then returns halloo
Upon the horizon amid adult enfantillages.

Its fire fails to pierce the vision that beholds it,
Fails to destroy the antique acceptances,
Except that the grandson sees it as it is,

Peter the voyant, who says "Mother, what is that"—
The object that rises with so much rhetoric,
But not for him. His question is complete.

It is the question of what he is capable.
It is the extreme, the expert aetat. 2.
He will never ride the red horse she describes.

His question is complete because it contains
His utmost statement. It is his own array,
His own pageant and procession and display,

As far as nothingness permits . . . Hear him.
He does not say, "Mother, my mother, who are you,"
The way the drowsy, infant, old men do.

AN ORDINARY EVENING IN NEW HAVEN

I

The eye's plain version is a thing apart,
The vulgate of experience. Of this,
A few words, an and yet, and yet, and yet—

As part of the never-ending meditation,
Part of the question that is a giant himself:
Of what is this house composed if not of the sun,

These houses, these difficult objects, dilapidate
Appearances of what appearances,
Words, lines, not meanings, not communications,

Dark things without a double, after all,
Unless a second giant kills the first—
A recent imagining of reality,

Much like a new resemblance of the sun,
Down-pouring, up-springing and inevitable,
A larger poem for a larger audience,

As if the crude collops came together as one,
A mythological form, a festival sphere,
A great bosom, beard and being, alive with age.

II

Suppose these houses are composed of ourselves,
So that they become an impalpable town, full of
Impalpable bells, transparencies of sound,

Sounding in transparent dwellings of the self,
Impalpable habitations that seem to move
In the movement of the colors of the mind,

The far-fire flowing and the dim-coned bells
Coming together in a sense in which we are poised,
Without regard to time or where we are,

In the perpetual reference, object
Of the perpetual meditation, point
Of the enduring, visionary love,

Obscure, in colors whether of the sun
Or mind, uncertain in the clearest bells,
The spirit's speeches, the indefinite,

Confused illuminations and sonorities,
So much ourselves, we cannot tell apart
The idea and the bearer-being of the idea.

III

The point of vision and desire are the same.
It is to the hero of midnight that we pray
On a hill of stones to make beau mont thereof.

If it is misery that infuriates our love,
If the black of night stands glistening on beau mont,
Then, ancientest saint ablaze with ancientest truth,

Say next to holiness is the will thereto,
And next to love is the desire for love,
The desire for its celestial ease in the heart,

Which nothing can frustrate, that most secure,
Unlike love in possession of that which was
To be possessed and is. But this cannot

Possess. It is desire, set deep in the eye,
Behind all actual seeing, in the actual scene,
In the street, in a room, on a carpet or a wall,

Always in emptiness that would be filled,
In denial that cannot contain its blood,
A porcelain, as yet in the bats thereof.

IV

The plainness of plain things is savagery,
As: the last plainness of a man who has fought
Against illusion and was, in a great grinding

Of growling teeth, and falls at night, snuffed out
By the obese opiates of sleep. Plain men in plain towns
Are not precise about the appeasement they need.

They only know a savage assuagement cries
With a savage voice; and in that cry they hear
Themselves transposed, muted and comforted

In a savage and subtle and simple harmony,
A matching and mating of surprised accords,
A responding to a diviner opposite.

So lewd spring comes from winter's chastity.
So, after summer, in the autumn air,
Comes the cold volume of forgotten ghosts,

But soothingly, with pleasant instruments,
So that this cold, a children's tale of ice,
Seems like a sheen of heat romanticized.

V

Inescapable romance, inescapable choice
Of dreams, disillusion as the last illusion,
Reality as a thing seen by the mind,

Not that which is but that which is apprehended,
A mirror, a lake of reflections in a room,
A glassy ocean lying at the door,

A great town hanging pendent in a shade,
An enormous nation happy in a style,
Everything as unreal as real can be,

In the inexquisite eye. Why, then, inquire
Who has divided the world, what entrepreneur?
No man. The self, the chrysalis of all men

Became divided in the leisure of blue day
And more, in branchings after day. One part
Held fast tenaciously in common earth

And one from central earth to central sky
And in moonlit extensions of them in the mind
Searched out such majesty as it could find.

VI

Reality is the beginning not the end,
Naked Alpha, not the hierophant Omega,
Of dense investiture, with luminous vassals.

It is the infant A standing on infant legs,
Not twisted, stooping, polymathic Z,
He that kneels always on the edge of space

In the pallid perceptions of its distances.
Alpha fears men or else Omega's men
Or else his prolongations of the human.

These characters are around us in the scene.
For one it is enough; for one it is not;
For neither is it profound absentia,

Since both alike appoint themselves the choice
Custodians of the glory of the scene,
The immaculate interpreters of life.

But that's the difference: in the end and the way
To the end. Alpha continues to begin.
Omega is refreshed at every end.

    VII

In the presence of such chapels and such schools,
The impoverished architects appear to be
Much richer, more fecund, sportive and alive.

The objects tingle and the spectator moves
With the objects. But the spectator also moves
With lesser things, with things exteriorized

Out of rigid realists. It is as if
Men turning into things, as comedy,
Stood, dressed in antic symbols, to display

The truth about themselves, having lost, as things,
That power to conceal they had as men,
Not merely as to depth but as to height

As well, not merely as to the commonplace
But, also, as to their miraculous,
Conceptions of new mornings of new worlds,

The tips of cock-cry pinked out pastily,
As that which was incredible becomes,
In misted contours, credible day again.

VIII

We fling ourselves, constantly longing, on this form.
We descend to the street and inhale a health of air
To our sepulchral hollows. Love of the real

Is soft in three-four cornered fragrances
From five-six cornered leaves, and green, the signal
To the lover, and blue, as of a secret place

In the anonymous color of the universe.
Our breath is like a desperate element
That we must calm, the origin of a mother tongue

With which to speak to her, the capable
In the midst of foreignness, the syllable
Of recognition, avowal, impassioned cry,

The cry that contains its converse in itself,
In which looks and feelings mingle and are part
As a quick answer modifies a question,

Not wholly spoken in a conversation between
Two bodies disembodied in their talk,
Too fragile, too immediate for any speech.

IX

We keep coming back and coming back
To the real: to the hotel instead of the hymns
That fall upon it out of the wind. We seek

The poem of pure reality, untouched
By trope or deviation, straight to the word,
Straight to the transfixing object, to the object

At the exactest point at which it is itself,
Transfixing by being purely what it is,
A view of New Haven, say, through the certain eye,

The eye made clear of uncertainty, with the sight
Of simple seeing, without reflection. We seek
Nothing beyond reality. Within it,

Everything, the spirit's alchemicana
Included, the spirit that goes roundabout
And through included, not merely the visible,

The solid, but the movable, the moment,
The coming on of feasts and the habits of saints,
The pattern of the heavens and high, night air.

X

It is fatal in the moon and empty there.
But, here, allons. The enigmatical
Beauty of each beautiful enigma

Becomes amassed in a total double-thing.
We do not know what is real and what is not.
We say of the moon, it is haunted by the man

Of bronze whose mind was made up and who, therefore, died.
We are not men of bronze and we are not dead.
His spirit is imprisoned in constant change.

But ours is not imprisoned. It resides
In a permanence composed of impermanence,
In a faithfulness as against the lunar light,

So that morning and evening are like promises kept,
So that the approaching sun and its arrival,
Its evening feast and the following festival,

This faithfulness of reality, this mode,
This tendance and venerable holding-in
Make gay the hallucinations in surfaces.

XI

In the metaphysical streets of the physical town
We remember the lion of Juda and we save
The phrase . . . Say of each lion of the spirit

It is a cat of a sleek transparency
That shines with a nocturnal shine alone.
The great cat must stand potent in the sun.

The phrase grows weak. The fact takes up the strength
Of the phrase. It contrives the self-same evocations
And Juda becomes New Haven or else must.

In the metaphysical streets, the profoundest forms
Go with the walker subtly walking there.
These he destroys with wafts of wakening,

Free from their majesty and yet in need
Of majesty, of an invincible clou,
A minimum of making in the mind,

A verity of the most veracious men,
The propounding of four seasons and twelve months,
The brilliancy at the central of the earth.

XII

The poem is the cry of its occasion,
Part of the res itself and not about it.
The poet speaks the poem as it is,

Not as it was: part of the reverberation
Of a windy night as it is, when the marble statues
Are like newspapers blown by the wind. He speaks

By sight and insight as they are. There is no
Tomorrow for him. The wind will have passed by,
The statues will have gone back to be things about.

The mobile and the immobile flickering
In the area between is and was are leaves,
Leaves burnished in autumnal burnished trees

And leaves in whirlings in the gutters, whirlings
Around and away, resembling the presence of thought,
Resembling the presences of thoughts, as if,

In the end, in the whole psychology, the self,
The town, the weather, in a casual litter,
Together, said words of the world are the life of the world.

XIII

The ephebe is solitary in his walk.
He skips the journalism of subjects, seeks out
The perquisites of sanctity, enjoys

A strong mind in a weak neighborhood and is
A serious man without the serious,
Inactive in his singular respect.

He is neither priest nor proctor at low eve,
Under the birds, among the perilous owls,
In the big X of the returning primitive.

It is a fresh spiritual that he defines,
A coldness in a long, too-constant warmth,
A thing on the side of a house, not deep in a cloud,

A difficulty that we predicate:
The difficulty of the visible
To the nations of the clear invisible,

The actual landscape with its actual horns
Of baker and butcher blowing, as if to hear,
Hear hard, gets at an essential integrity.

XIV

The dry eucalyptus seeks god in the rainy cloud.
Professor Eucalyptus of New Haven seeks him
In New Haven with an eye that does not look

Beyond the object. He sits in his room, beside
The window, close to the ramshackle spout in which
The rain falls with a ramshackle sound. He seeks

God in the object itself, without much choice.
It is a choice of the commodious adjective
For what he sees, it comes in the end to that:

The description that makes it divinity, still speech
As it touches the point of reverberation—not grim
Reality but reality grimly seen

And spoken in paradisal parlance new
And in any case never grim, the human grim
That is part of the indifference of the eye

Indifferent to what it sees. The tink-tonk
Of the rain in the spout is not a substitute.
It is of the essence not yet well perceived.

    xv

He preserves himself against the repugnant rain
By an instinct for a rainless land, the self
Of his self, come at upon wide delvings of wings.

The instinct for heaven had its counterpart:
The instinct for earth, for New Haven, for his room,
The gay tournamonde as of a single world

In which he is and as and is are one.
For its counterpart a kind of counterpoint
Irked the wet wallows of the water-spout.

The rain kept falling loudly in the trees
And on the ground. The hibernal dark that hung
In primavera, the shadow of bare rock,

Becomes the rock of autumn, glittering,
Ponderable source of each imponderable,
The weight we lift with the finger of a dream,

The heaviness we lighten by light will,
By the hand of desire, faint, sensitive, the soft
Touch and trouble of the touch of the actual hand.

XVI

Among time's images, there is not one
Of this present, the venerable mask above
The dilapidation of dilapidations.

The oldest-newest day is the newest alone.
The oldest-newest night does not creak by,
With lanterns, like a celestial ancientness.

Silently it heaves its youthful sleep from the sea—
The Oklahoman—the Italian blue
Beyond the horizon with its masculine,

Their eyes closed, in a young palaver of lips.
And yet the wind whimpers oldly of old age
In the western night. The venerable mask,

In this perfection, occasionally speaks
And something of death's poverty is heard.
This should be tragedy's most moving face.

It is a bough in the electric light
And exhalations in the eaves, so little
To indicate the total leaflessness.

XVII

The color is almost the color of comedy,
Not quite. It comes to the point and at the point,
It fails. The strength at the center is serious.

Perhaps instead of failing it rejects
As a serious strength rejects pin-idleness.
A blank underlies the trials of device,

The dominant blank, the unapproachable.
This is the mirror of the high serious:
Blue verdured into a damask's lofty symbol,

Gold easings and ouncings and fluctuations of thread
And beetling of belts and lights of general stones,
Like blessed beams from out a blessed bush

Or the wasted figurations of the wastes
Of night, time and the imagination,
Saved and beholden, in a robe of rays.

These fitful sayings are, also, of tragedy:
The serious reflection is composed
Neither of comic nor tragic but of commonplace.

XVIII

It is the window that makes it difficult
To say good-by to the past and to live and to be
In the present state of things as, say, to paint

In the present state of painting and not the state
Of thirty years ago. It is looking out
Of the window and walking in the street and seeing,

As if the eyes were the present or part of it,
As if the ears heard any shocking sound,
As if life and death were ever physical.

The life and death of this carpenter depend
On a fuchsia in a can—and iridescences
Of petals that will never be realized,

Things not yet true which he perceives through truth,
Or thinks he does, as he perceives the present,
Or thinks he does, a carpenter's iridescences,

Wooden, the model for astral apprentices,
A city slapped up like a chest of tools,
The eccentric exterior of which the clocks talk.

                XIX

The moon rose in the mind and each thing there
Picked up its radial aspect in the night,
Prostrate below the singleness of its will.

That which was public green turned private gray.
At another time, the radial aspect came
From a different source. But there was always one:

A century in which everything was part
Of that century and of its aspect, a personage,
A man who was the axis of his time,

An image that begot its infantines,
Imaginary poles whose intelligence
Streamed over chaos their civilities.

What is the radial aspect of this place,
This present colony of a colony
Of colonies, a sense in the changing sense

Of things? A figure like Ecclesiast,
Rugged and luminous, chants in the dark
A text that is an answer, although obscure.

XX

The imaginative transcripts were like clouds,
Today; and the transcripts of feeling, impossible
To distinguish. The town was a residuum,

A neuter shedding shapes in an absolute.
Yet the transcripts of it when it was blue remain;
And the shapes that it took in feeling, the persons that

It became, the nameless, flitting characters—
These actors still walk in a twilight muttering lines.
It may be that they mingle, clouds and men, in the air

Or street or about the corners of a man,
Who sits thinking in the corners of a room.
In this chamber the pure sphere escapes the impure,

Because the thinker himself escapes. And yet
To have evaded clouds and men leaves him
A naked being with a naked will

And everything to make. He may evade
Even his own will and in his nakedness
Inhabit the hypnosis of that sphere.

XXI

But he may not. He may not evade his will,
Nor the wills of other men; and he cannot evade
The will of necessity, the will of wills—

Romanza out of the black shepherd's isle,
Like the constant sound of the water of the sea
In the hearing of the shepherd and his black forms;

Out of the isle, but not of any isle.
Close to the senses there lies another isle
And there the senses give and nothing take,

The opposite of Cythère, an isolation
At the center, the object of the will, this place,
The things around—the alternate romanza

Out of the surfaces, the windows, the walls,
The bricks grown brittle in time's poverty,
The clear. A celestial mode is paramount,

If only in the branches sweeping in the rain:
The two romanzas, the distant and the near,
Are a single voice in the boo-ha of the wind.

XXII

Professor Eucalyptus said, "The search
For reality is as momentous as
The search for god." It is the philosopher's search

For an interior made exterior
And the poet's search for the same exterior made
Interior: breathless things broodingly abreath

With the inhalations of original cold
And of original earliness. Yet the sense
Of cold and earliness is a daily sense,

Not the predicate of bright origin.
Creation is not renewed by images
Of lone wanderers. To re-create, to use

The cold and earliness and bright origin
Is to search. Likewise to say of the evening star,
The most ancient light in the most ancient sky,

That it is wholly an inner light, that it shines
From the sleepy bosom of the real, re-creates,
Searches a possible for its possibleness.

XXIII

The sun is half the world, half everything,
The bodiless half. There is always this bodiless half,
This illumination, this elevation, this future

Or, say, the late going colors of that past,
Effete green, the woman in black cassimere.
If, then, New Haven is half sun, what remains,

At evening, after dark, is the other half,
Lighted by space, big over those that sleep,
Of the single future of night, the single sleep,

As of a long, inevitable sound,
A kind of cozening and coaxing sound,
And the goodness of lying in a maternal sound,

Unfretted by day's separate, several selves,
Being part of everything come together as one.
In this identity, disembodiments

Still keep occurring. What is, uncertainly,
Desire prolongs its adventure to create
Forms of farewell, furtive among green ferns.

XXIV

The consolations of space are nameless things.
It was after the neurosis of winter. It was
In the genius of summer that they blew up

The statue of Jove among the boomy clouds.
It took all day to quieten the sky
And then to refill its emptiness again,

So that at the edge of afternoon, not over,
Before the thought of evening had occurred
Or the sound of Incomincia had been set,

There was a clearing, a readiness for first bells,
An opening for outpouring, the hand was raised:
There was a willingness not yet composed,

A knowing that something certain had been proposed,
Which, without the statue, would be new,
An escape from repetition, a happening

In space and the self, that touched them both at once
And alike, a point of the sky or of the earth
Or of a town poised at the horizon's dip.

Life fixed him, wandering on the stair of glass,
With its attentive eyes. And, as he stood,
On his balcony, outsensing distances,

There were looks that caught him out of empty air.
C'est toujours la vie qui me regarde . . . This was
Who watched him, always, for unfaithful thought.

This sat beside his bed, with its guitar,
To keep him from forgetting, without a word,
A note or two disclosing who it was.

Nothing about him ever stayed the same,
Except this hidalgo and his eye and tune,
The shawl across one shoulder and the hat.

The commonplace became a rumpling of blazons.
What was real turned into something most unreal,
Bare beggar-tree, hung low for fruited red

In isolated moments—isolations
Were false. The hidalgo was permanent, abstract,
A hatching that stared and demanded an answering look.

XXVI

How facilely the purple blotches fell
On the walk, purple and blue, and red and gold,
Blooming and beaming and voluming colors out.

Away from them, capes, along the afternoon Sound,
Shook off their dark marine in lapis light.
The sea shivered in transcendent change, rose up

As rain and booming, gleaming, blowing, swept
The wateriness of green wet in the sky.
Mountains appeared with greater eloquence

Than that of their clouds. These lineaments were the earth,
Seen as inamorata, of loving fame
Added and added out of a fame-full heart . . .

But, here, the inamorata, without distance
And thereby lost, and naked or in rags,
Shrunk in the poverty of being close,

Touches, as one hand touches another hand,
Or as a voice that, speaking without form,
Gritting the ear, whispers humane repose.

    XXVII

A scholar, in his Segmenta, left a note,
As follows, "The Ruler of Reality,
If more unreal than New Haven, is not

A real ruler, but rules what is unreal."
In addition, there were draftings of him, thus:
"He is the consort of the Queen of Fact.

Sunrise is his garment's hem, sunset is hers.
He is the theorist of life, not death,
The total excellence of its total book."

Again, "The sibilance of phrases is his
Or partly his. His voice is audible,
As the fore-meaning in music is." Again,

"This man abolishes by being himself
That which is not ourselves: the regalia,
The attributions, the plume and helmet-ho."

Again, "He has thought it out, he thinks it out,
As he has been and is and, with the Queen
Of Fact, lies at his ease beside the sea."

XXVIII

If it should be true that reality exists
In the mind: the tin plate, the loaf of bread on it,
The long-bladed knife, the little to drink and her

Misericordia, it follows that
Real and unreal are two in one: New Haven
Before and after one arrives or, say,

Bergamo on a postcard, Rome after dark,
Sweden described, Salzburg with shaded eyes
Or Paris in conversation at a café.

This endlessly elaborating poem
Displays the theory of poetry,
As the life of poetry. A more severe,

More harassing master would extemporize
Subtler, more urgent proof that the theory
Of poetry is the theory of life,

As it is, in the intricate evasions of as,
In things seen and unseen, created from nothingness,
The heavens, the hells, the worlds, the longed-for lands.

XXIX

In the land of the lemon trees, yellow and yellow were
Yellow-blue, yellow-green, pungent with citron-sap,
Dangling and spangling, the mic-mac of mocking birds.

In the land of the elm trees, wandering mariners
Looked on big women, whose ruddy-ripe images
Wreathed round and round the round wreath of autumn.

They rolled their r's, there, in the land of the citrons.
In the land of big mariners, the words they spoke
Were mere brown clods, mere catching weeds of talk.

When the mariners came to the land of the lemon trees,
At last, in that blond atmosphere, bronzed hard,
They said, "We are back once more in the land of the elm trees,

But folded over, turned round." It was the same,
Except for the adjectives, an alteration
Of words that was a change of nature, more

Than the difference that clouds make over a town.
The countrymen were changed and each constant thing.
Their dark-colored words had redescribed the citrons.

XXX

The last leaf that is going to fall has fallen.
The robins are là-bas, the squirrels, in tree-caves,
Huddle together in the knowledge of squirrels.

The wind has blown the silence of summer away.
It buzzes beyond the horizon or in the ground:
In mud under ponds, where the sky used to be reflected.

The barrenness that appears is an exposing.
It is not part of what is absent, a halt
For farewells, a sad hanging on for remembrances.

It is a coming on and a coming forth.
The pines that were fans and fragrances emerge,
Staked solidly in a gusty grappling with rocks.

The glass of the air becomes an element—
It was something imagined that has been washed away.
A clearness has returned. It stands restored.

It is not an empty clearness, a bottomless sight.
It is a visibility of thought,
In which hundreds of eyes, in one mind, see at once.

XXXI

The less legible meanings of sounds, the little reds
Not often realized, the lighter words
In the heavy drum of speech, the inner men

Behind the outer shields, the sheets of music
In the strokes of thunder, dead candles at the window
When day comes, fire-foams in the motions of the sea,

Flickings from finikin to fine finikin
And the general fidget from busts of Constantine
To photographs of the late president, Mr. Blank,

These are the edgings and inchings of final form,
The swarming activities of the formulae
Of statement, directly and indirectly getting at,

Like an evening evoking the spectrum of violet,
A philosopher practicing scales on his piano,
A woman writing a note and tearing it up.

It is not in the premise that reality
Is a solid. It may be a shade that traverses
A dust, a force that traverses a shade.

ANGEL SURROUNDED BY PAYSANS

One of the countrymen:

                                        There is
        A welcome at the door to which no one comes?
The angel:
        I am the angel of reality,
        Seen for a moment standing in the door.

        I have neither ashen wing nor wear of ore
        And live without a tepid aureole,

        Or stars that follow me, not to attend,
        But, of my being and its knowing, part.

        I am one of you and being one of you
        Is being and knowing what I am and know.

        Yet I am the necessary angel of earth,
        Since, in my sight, you see the earth again,

        Cleared of its stiff and stubborn, man-locked set,
        And, in my hearing, you hear its tragic drone

        Rise liquidly in liquid lingerings,
        Like watery words awash; like meanings said

        By repetitions of half-meanings. Am I not,
        Myself, only half of a figure of a sort,

        A figure half seen, or seen for a moment, a man
        Of the mind, an apparition apparelled in

        Apparels of such lightest look that a turn
        Of my shoulder and quickly, too quickly, I am gone?

SOMEONE PUTS A PINEAPPLE TOGETHER

I

O juventes, O filii, he contemplates
A wholly artificial nature, in which
The profusion of metaphor has been increased.

It is something on a table that he sees,
The root of a form, as of this fruit, a fund,
The angel at the center of this rind,

This husk of Cuba, tufted emerald,
Himself, may be, the irreducible X
At the bottom of imagined artifice,

Its inhabitant and elect expositor.
It is as if there were three planets: the sun,
The moon and the imagination, or, say,

Day, night and man and his endless effigies.
If he sees an object on a table, much like
A jar of the shoots of an infant country, green

And bright, or like a venerable urn,
Which, from the ash within it, fortifies
A green that is the ash of what green is,

He sees it in this tangent of himself.
And in this tangent it becomes a thing
Of weight, on which the weightless rests: from which

The ephemeras of the tangent swarm, the chance
Concourse of planetary originals,
Yet, as it seems, of human residence.

II

He must say nothing of the fruit that is
Not true, nor think it, less. He must defy
The metaphor that murders metaphor.

He seeks as image a second of the self,
Made subtle by truth's most jealous subtlety,
Like the true light of the truest sun, the true

Power in the waving of the wand of the moon,
Whose shining is the intelligence of our sleep.
He seeks an image certain as meaning is

To sound, sound's substance and executant,
The particular tingle in a proclamation
That makes it say the little thing it says,

Below the prerogative jumble. The fruit so seen
As a part of the nature that he contemplates
Is fertile with more than changes of the light

On the table or in the colors of the room.
Its propagations are more erudite,
Like precious scholia jotted down in the dark.

Did not the age that bore him bear him among
Its infiltrations? There had been an age
When a pineapple on the table was enough,

Without the forfeit scholar coming in,
Without his enlargings and pale arrondissements,
Without the furious roar in his capital.

Green had, those days, its own implacable sting.
But now a habit of the truth had formed
To protect him in a privacy, in which

The scholar, captious, told him what he could
Of there, where the truth was not the respect of one,
But always of many things. He had not to be told

Of the incredible subjects of poetry.
He was willing they should remain incredible,
Because the incredible, also, has its truth,

Its tuft of emerald that is real, for all
Its invitation to false metaphor.
The incredible gave him a purpose to believe.

III

How thick this gobbet is with overlays,
The double fruit of boisterous epicures,
Like the same orange repeating on one tree

A single self. Divest reality
Of its propriety. Admit the shaft
Of that third planet to the table and then:

1. The hut stands by itself beneath the palms.
2. Out of their bottle the green genii come.
3. A vine has climbed the other side of the wall.

4. The sea is spouting upward out of rocks.
5. The symbol of feasts and of oblivion . . .
6. White sky, pink sun, trees on a distant peak.

7. These lozenges are nailed-up lattices.
8. The owl sits humped. It has a hundred eyes.
9. The coconut and cockerel in one.

10. This is how yesterday's volcano looks.
11. There is an island Palahude by name—
12. An uncivil shape like a gigantic haw.

These casual exfoliations are
Of the tropic of resemblance, sprigs
Of Capricorn or as the sign demands,

Apposites, to the slightest edge, of the whole
Undescribed composition of the sugar-cone,
Shiftings of an inchoate crystal tableau,

The momentary footings of a climb
Up the pineapple, a table Alp and yet
An Alp, a purple Southern mountain bisqued

With the molten mixings of related things,
Cat's taste possibly or possibly Danish lore,
The small luxuriations that portend

Universal delusions of universal grandeurs,
The slight incipiencies, of which the form,
At last, is the pineapple on the table or else

An object the sum of its complications, seen
And unseen. This is everybody's world.
Here the total artifice reveals itself

As the total reality. Therefore it is
One says even of the odor of this fruit,
That steeps the room, quickly, then not at all,

It is more than the odor of this core of earth
And water. It is that which is distilled
In the prolific ellipses that we know,

In the planes that tilt hard revelations on
The eye, a geometric glitter, tiltings
As of sections collecting toward the greenest cone.

THE PLAIN SENSE OF THINGS

After the leaves have fallen, we return
To a plain sense of things. It is as if
We had come to an end of the imagination,
Inanimate in an inert savoir.

It is difficult even to choose the adjective
For this blank cold, this sadness without cause.
The great structure has become a minor house.
No turban walks across the lessened floors.

The greenhouse never so badly needed paint.
The chimney is fifty years old and slants to one side.
A fantastic effort has failed, a repetition
In a repetitiousness of men and flies.

Yet the absence of the imagination had
Itself to be imagined. The great pond,
The plain sense of it, without reflections, leaves,
Mud, water like dirty glass, expressing silence

Of a sort, silence of a rat come out to see,
The great pond and its waste of the lilies, all this
Had to be imagined as an inevitable knowledge,
Required, as a necessity requires.

LEBENSWEISHEITSPIELEREI

Weaker and weaker, the sunlight falls
In the afternoon. The proud and the strong
Have departed.

Those that are left are the unaccomplished,
The finally human,
Natives of a dwindled sphere.

Their indigence is an indigence
That is an indigence of the light,
A stellar pallor that hangs on the threads.

Little by little, the poverty
Of autumnal space becomes
A look, a few words spoken.

Each person completely touches us
With what he is and as he is,
In the stale grandeur of annihilation.

THE HERMITAGE AT THE CENTER

The leaves on the macadam make a noise—
  How soft the grass on which the desired
  Reclines in the temperature of heaven—

Like tales that were told the day before yesterday—
  Sleek in a natural nakedness,
  She attends the tintinnabula—

And the wind sways like a great thing tottering—
  Of birds called up by more than the sun,
  Birds of more wit, that substitute—

Which suddenly is all dissolved and gone—
  Their intelligible twittering
  For unintelligible thought.

And yet this end and this beginning are one,
  And one last look at the ducks is a look
  At lucent children round her in a ring.

THE GREEN PLANT

Silence is a shape that has passed.
Otu-bre's lion-roses have turned to paper
And the shadows of the trees
Are like wrecked umbrellas.

The effete vocabulary of summer
No longer says anything.
The brown at the bottom of red,
The orange far down in yellow,

Are falsifications from a sun
In a mirror, without heat,
In a constant secondariness,
A turning down toward finality—

Except that a green plant glares, as you look
At the legend of the maroon and olive forest,
Glares, outside of the legend, with the barbarous green
Of the harsh reality of which it is part.

MADAME LA FLEURIE

Weight him down, O side-stars, with the great weightings of the end.
Seal him there. He looked in a glass of the earth and thought he lived in it.
Now, he brings all that he saw into the earth, to the waiting parent.
His crisp knowledge is devoured by her, beneath a dew.

Weight him, weight, weight him with the sleepiness of the moon.
It was only a glass because he looked in it. It was nothing he could be told.
It was a language he spoke, because he must, yet did not know.
It was a page he had found in the handbook of heartbreak.

The black fugatos are strumming the blacknesses of black . . .
The thick strings stutter the finial gutturals.
He does not lie there remembering the blue-jay, say the jay.
His grief is that his mother should feed on him, himself and what he saw,
In that distant chamber, a bearded queen, wicked in her dead light.

TO AN OLD PHILOSOPHER IN ROME

On the threshold of heaven, the figures in the street
Become the figures of heaven, the majestic movement
Of men growing small in the distances of space,
Singing, with smaller and still smaller sound,
Unintelligible absolution and an end—

The threshold, Rome, and that more merciful Rome
Beyond, the two alike in the make of the mind.
It is as if in a human dignity
Two parallels become one, a perspective, of which
Men are part both in the inch and in the mile.

How easily the blown banners change to wings . . .
Things dark on the horizons of perception,
Become accompaniments of fortune, but
Of the fortune of the spirit, beyond the eye,
Not of its sphere, and yet not far beyond,

The human end in the spirit's greatest reach,
The extreme of the known in the presence of the extreme
Of the unknown. The newsboys' muttering
Becomes another murmuring; the smell
Of medicine, a fragrantness not to be spoiled . . .

The bed, the books, the chair, the moving nuns,
The candle as it evades the sight, these are
The sources of happiness in the shape of Rome,
A shape within the ancient circles of shapes,
And these beneath the shadow of a shape

In a confusion on bed and books, a portent
On the chair, a moving transparence on the nuns,
A light on the candle tearing against the wick
To join a hovering excellence, to escape
From fire and be part only of that of which

Fire is the symbol: the celestial possible.
Speak to your pillow as if it was yourself.
Be orator but with an accurate tongue
And without eloquence, O, half-asleep,
Of the pity that is the memorial of this room,

So that we feel, in this illumined large,
The veritable small, so that each of us
Beholds himself in you, and hears his voice
In yours, master and commiserable man,
Intent on your particles of nether-do,

Your dozing in the depths of wakefulness,
In the warmth of your bed, at the edge of your chair, alive
Yet living in two worlds, impenitent
As to one, and, as to one, most penitent,
Impatient for the grandeur that you need

In so much misery; and yet finding it
Only in misery, the afflatus of ruin,
Profound poetry of the poor and of the dead,
As in the last drop of the deepest blood,
As it falls from the heart and lies there to be seen,

Even as the blood of an empire, it might be,
For a citizen of heaven though still of Rome.
It is poverty's speech that seeks us out the most.
It is older than the oldest speech of Rome.
This is the tragic accent of the scene.

And you—it is you that speak it, without speech,
The loftiest syllables among loftiest things,
The one invulnerable man among
Crude captains, the naked majesty, if you like,
Of bird-nest arches and of rain-stained vaults.

The sounds drift in. The buildings are remembered.
The life of the city never lets go, nor do you
Ever want it to. It is part of the life in your room.
Its domes are the architecture of your bed.
The bells keep on repeating solemn names

In choruses and choirs of choruses,
Unwilling that mercy should be a mystery
Of silence, that any solitude of sense
Should give you more than their peculiar chords
And reverberations clinging to whisper still.

It is a kind of total grandeur at the end,
With every visible thing enlarged and yet
No more than a bed, a chair and moving nuns,
The immensest theatre, the pillared porch,
The book and candle in your ambered room,

Total grandeur of a total edifice,
Chosen by an inquisitor of structures
For himself. He stops upon this threshold,
As if the design of all his words takes form
And frame from thinking and is realized.

VACANCY IN THE PARK

March . . . Someone has walked across the snow,
Someone looking for he knows not what.

It is like a boat that has pulled away
From a shore at night and disappeared.

It is like a guitar left on a table
By a woman, who has forgotten it.

It is like the feeling of a man
Come back to see a certain house.

The four winds blow through the rustic arbor,
Under its mattresses of vines.

THE POEM THAT TOOK THE PLACE OF A MOUNTAIN

There it was, word for word,
The poem that took the place of a mountain.

He breathed its oxygen,
Even when the book lay turned in the dust of his table.

It reminded him how he had needed
A place to go to in his own direction,

How he had recomposed the pines,
Shifted the rocks and picked his way among clouds,

For the outlook that would be right,
Where he would be complete in an unexplained completion:

The exact rock where his inexactnesses
Would discover, at last, the view toward which they had edged,

Where he could lie and, gazing down at the sea,
Recognize his unique and solitary home.

TWO ILLUSTRATIONS THAT THE WORLD
IS WHAT YOU MAKE OF IT

I
THE CONSTANT DISQUISITION OF THE WIND

The sky seemed so small that winter day,
A dirty light on a lifeless world,
Contracted like a withered stick.

It was not the shadow of cloud and cold,
But a sense of the distance of the sun—
The shadow of a sense of his own,

A knowledge that the actual day
Was so much less. Only the wind
Seemed large and loud and high and strong.

And as he thought within the thought
Of the wind, not knowing that that thought
Was not his thought, nor anyone's,

The appropriate image of himself,
So formed, became himself and he breathed
The breath of another nature as his own,

But only its momentary breath,
Outside of and beyond the dirty light,
That never could be animal,

A nature still without a shape,
Except his own—perhaps, his own
In a Sunday's violent idleness.

II

THE WORLD IS LARGER IN SUMMER

He left half a shoulder and half a head
To recognize him in after time.

These marbles lay weathering in the grass
When the summer was over, when the change

Of summer and of the sun, the life
Of summer and of the sun, were gone.

He had said that everything possessed
The power to transform itself, or else,

And what meant more, to be transformed.
He discovered the colors of the moon

In a single spruce, when, suddenly,
The tree stood dazzling in the air

And blue broke on him from the sun,
A bullioned blue, a blue abulge,

Like daylight, with time's bellishings,
And sensuous summer stood full-height.

The master of the spruce, himself,
Became transformed. But his mastery

Left only the fragments found in the grass,
From his project, as finally magnified.

PROLOGUES TO WHAT IS POSSIBLE

I

There was an ease of mind that was like being alone in a boat at sea,
A boat carried forward by waves resembling the bright backs of rowers,
Gripping their oars, as if they were sure of the way to their destination,
Bending over and pulling themselves erect on the wooden handles,
Wet with water and sparkling in the one-ness of their motion.

The boat was built of stones that had lost their weight and being no longer heavy
Had left in them only a brilliance, of unaccustomed origin,
So that he that stood up in the boat leaning and looking before him
Did not pass like someone voyaging out of and beyond the familiar.
He belonged to the far-foreign departure of his vessel and was part of it,
Part of the speculum of fire on its prow, its symbol, whatever it was,
Part of the glass-like sides on which it glided over the salt-stained water,
As he traveled alone, like a man lured on by a syllable without any meaning,
A syllable of which he felt, with an appointed sureness,
That it contained the meaning into which he wanted to enter,
A meaning which, as he entered it, would shatter the boat and leave the oarsmen quiet
As at a point of central arrival, an instant moment, much or little,
Removed from any shore, from any man or woman, and needing none.

II

The metaphor stirred his fear. The object with which he was compared
Was beyond his recognizing. By this he knew that likeness of him extended
Only a little way, and not beyond, unless between himself
And things beyond resemblance there was this and that intended to be recognized,
The this and that in the enclosures of hypotheses
On which men speculated in summer when they were half asleep.

What self, for example, did he contain that had not yet been loosed,
Snarling in him for discovery as his attentions spread,
As if all his hereditary lights were suddenly increased
By an access of color, a new and unobserved, slight dithering,
The smallest lamp, which added its puissant flick, to which he gave
A name and privilege over the ordinary of his commonplace—

A flick which added to what was real and its vocabulary,
The way some first thing coming into Northern trees
Adds to them the whole vocabulary of the South,
The way the earliest single light in the evening sky, in spring,
Creates a fresh universe out of nothingness by adding itself,
The way a look or a touch reveals its unexpected magnitudes.

SONG OF FIXED ACCORD

Rou-cou spoke the dove,
Like the sooth lord of sorrow,
Of sooth love and sorrow,
And a hail-bow, hail-bow,
To this morrow.

She lay upon the roof,
A little wet of wing and woe,
And she rou-ed there,
Softly she piped among the suns
And their ordinary glare,

The sun of five, the sun of six,
Their ordinariness,
And the ordinariness of seven,
Which she accepted,
Like a fixed heaven,

Not subject to change . . .
Day's invisible beginner,
The lord of love and of sooth sorrow,
Lay on the roof
And made much within her.

THE WORLD AS MEDITATION

J'ai passé trop de temps à travailler mon violon,
à voyager. Mais l'exercice essentiel du
compositeur—la méditation—rien ne l'a jamais
suspendu en moi . . . Je vis un rêve permanent,
qui ne s'arrête ni nuit ni jour.
　　　　　　　　　　　—GEORGES ENESCO

Is it Ulysses that approaches from the east,
The interminable adventurer? The trees are mended.
That winter is washed away. Someone is moving

On the horizon and lifting himself up above it.
A form of fire approaches the cretonnes of Penelope,
Whose mere savage presence awakens the world in which she dwells.

She has composed, so long, a self with which to welcome him,
Companion to his self for her, which she imagined,
Two in a deep-founded sheltering, friend and dear friend.

The trees had been mended, as an essential exercise
In an inhuman meditation, larger than her own.
No winds like dogs watched over her at night.

She wanted nothing he could not bring her by coming alone.
She wanted no fetchings. His arms would be her necklace
And her belt, the final fortune of their desire.

But was it Ulysses? Or was it only the warmth of the sun
On her pillow? The thought kept beating in her like her heart.
The two kept beating together. It was only day.

It was Ulysses and it was not. Yet they had met,
Friend and dear friend and a planet's encouragement.
The barbarous strength within her would never fail.

She would talk a little to herself as she combed her hair,
Repeating his name with its patient syllables,
Never forgetting him that kept coming constantly so near.

LONG AND SLUGGISH LINES

It makes so little difference, at so much more
Than seventy, where one looks, one has been there before.

Wood-smoke rises through trees, is caught in an upper flow
Of air and whirled away. But it has been often so.

The trees have a look as if they bore sad names
And kept saying over and over one same, same thing,

In a kind of uproar, because an opposite, a contradiction,
Has enraged them and made them want to talk it down.

What opposite? Could it be that yellow patch, the side
Of a house, that makes one think the house is laughing;

Or these—escent—issant pre-personae: first fly,
A comic infanta among the tragic drapings,

Babyishness of forsythia, a snatch of belief,
The spook and makings of the nude magnolia?

. . . Wanderer, this is the pre-history of February.
The life of the poem in the mind has not yet begun.

You were not born yet when the trees were crystal
Nor are you now, in this wakefulness inside a sleep.

A QUIET NORMAL LIFE

His place, as he sat and as he thought, was not
In anything that he constructed, so frail,
So barely lit, so shadowed over and naught,

As, for example, a world in which, like snow,
He became an inhabitant, obedient
To gallant notions on the part of cold.

It was here. This was the setting and the time
Of year. Here in his house and in his room,
In his chair, the most tranquil thought grew peaked

And the oldest and the warmest heart was cut
By gallant notions on the part of night—
Both late and alone, above the crickets' chords,

Babbling, each one, the uniqueness of its sound.
There was no fury in transcendent forms.
But his actual candle blazed with artifice.

FINAL SOLILOQUY OF THE INTERIOR PARAMOUR

Light the first light of evening, as in a room
In which we rest and, for small reason, think
The world imagined is the ultimate good.

This is, therefore, the intensest rendezvous.
It is in that thought that we collect ourselves,
Out of all the indifferences, into one thing:

Within a single thing, a single shawl
Wrapped tightly round us, since we are poor, a warmth,
A light, a power, the miraculous influence.

Here, now, we forget each other and ourselves.
We feel the obscurity of an order, a whole,
A knowledge, that which arranged the rendezvous,

Within its vital boundary, in the mind.
We say God and the imagination are one . . .
How high that highest candle lights the dark.

Out of this same light, out of the central mind,
We make a dwelling in the evening air,
In which being there together is enough.

THE ROCK

SEVENTY YEARS LATER

It is an illusion that we were ever alive,
Lived in the houses of mothers, arranged ourselves
By our own motions in a freedom of air.

Regard the freedom of seventy years ago.
It is no longer air. The houses still stand,
Though they are rigid in rigid emptiness.

Even our shadows, their shadows, no longer remain.
The lives these lived in the mind are at an end.
They never were . . . The sounds of the guitar

Were not and are not. Absurd. The words spoken
Were not and are not. It is not to be believed.
The meeting at noon at the edge of the field seems like

An invention, an embrace between one desperate clod
And another in a fantastic consciousness,
In a queer assertion of humanity:

A theorem proposed between the two—
Two figures in a nature of the sun,
In the sun's design of its own happiness,

As if nothingness contained a métier,
A vital assumption, an impermanence
In its permanent cold, an illusion so desired

That the green leaves came and covered the high rock,
That the lilacs came and bloomed, like a blindness cleaned,
Exclaiming bright sight, as it was satisfied,

In a birth of sight. The blooming and the musk
Were being alive, an incessant being alive,
A particular of being, that gross universe.

II

THE POEM AS ICON

It is not enough to cover the rock with leaves.
We must be cured of it by a cure of the ground
Or a cure of ourselves, that is equal to a cure

Of the ground, a cure beyond forgetfulness.
And yet the leaves, if they broke into bud,
If they broke into bloom, if they bore fruit,

And if we ate the incipient colorings
Of their fresh culls might be a cure of the ground.
The fiction of the leaves is the icon

Of the poem, the figuration of blessedness,
And the icon is the man. The pearled chaplet of spring,
The magnum wreath of summer, time's autumn snood,

Its copy of the sun, these cover the rock.
These leaves are the poem, the icon and the man.
These are a cure of the ground and of ourselves,

In the predicate that there is nothing else.
They bud and bloom and bear their fruit without change.
They are more than leaves that cover the barren rock.

They bud the whitest eye, the pallidest sprout,
New senses in the engenderings of sense,
The desire to be at the end of distances,

The body quickened and the mind in root.
They bloom as a man loves, as he lives in love.
They bear their fruit so that the year is known,

As if its understanding was brown skin,
The honey in its pulp, the final found,
The plenty of the year and of the world.

In this plenty, the poem makes meanings of the rock,
Of such mixed motion and such imagery
That its barrenness becomes a thousand things

And so exists no more. This is the cure
Of leaves and of the ground and of ourselves.
His words are both the icon and the man.

III

FORMS OF THE ROCK IN A NIGHT-HYMN

The rock is the gray particular of man's life,
The stone from which he rises, up—and—ho,
The step to the bleaker depths of his descents . . .

The rock is the stern particular of the air,
The mirror of the planets, one by one,
But through man's eye, their silent rhapsodist,

Turquoise the rock, at odious evening bright
With redness that sticks fast to evil dreams;
The difficult rightness of half-risen day.

The rock is the habitation of the whole,
Its strength and measure, that which is near, point A
In a perspective that begins again

At B: the origin of the mango's rind.
It is the rock where tranquil must adduce
Its tranquil self, the main of things, the mind,

The starting point of the human and the end,
That in which space itself is contained, the gate
To the enclosure, day, the things illumined

By day, night and that which night illumines,
Night and its midnight-minting fragrances,
Night's hymn of the rock, as in a vivid sleep.

ST. ARMORER'S CHURCH FROM THE OUTSIDE

St. Armorer's was once an immense success.
It rose loftily and stood massively; and to lie
In its church-yard, in the province of St. Armorer's,
Fixed one for good in geranium-colored day.

What is left has the foreign smell of plaster,
The closed-in smell of hay. A sumac grows
On the altar, growing toward the lights, inside.
Reverberations leak and lack among holes . . .

Its chapel rises from Terre Ensevelie,
An ember yes among its cindery noes,
His own: a chapel of breath, an appearance made
For a sign of meaning in the meaningless,

No radiance of dead blaze, but something seen
In a mystic eye, no sign of life but life,
Itself, the presence of the intelligible
In that which is created as its symbol.

It is like a new account of everything old,
Matisse at Vence and a great deal more than that,
A new-colored sun, say, that will soon change forms
And spread hallucinations on every leaf.

The chapel rises, his own, his period,
A civilization formed from the outward blank,
A sacred syllable rising from sacked speech,
The first car out of a tunnel en voyage

Into lands of ruddy-ruby fruits, achieved
Not merely desired, for sale, and market things
That press, strong peasants in a peasant world,
Their purports to a final seriousness—

Final for him, the acceptance of such prose,
Time's given perfections made to seem like less
Than the need of each generation to be itself,
The need to be actual and as it is.

St. Armorer's has nothing of this present,
This *vif,* this dizzle-dazzle of being new
And of becoming, for which the chapel spreads out
Its arches in its vivid element,

In the air of newness of that element,
In an air of freshness, clearness, greenness, blueness,
That which is always beginning because it is part
Of that which is always beginning, over and over.

The chapel underneath St. Armorer's walls,
Stands in a light, its natural light and day,
The origin and keep of its health and his own.
And there he walks and does as he lives and likes.

THE PLANET ON THE TABLE

Ariel was glad he had written his poems.
They were of a remembered time
Or of something seen that he liked.

Other makings of the sun
Were waste and welter
And the ripe shrub writhed.

His self and the sun were one
And his poems, although makings of his self,
Were no less makings of the sun.

It was not important that they survive.
What mattered was that they should bear
Some lineament or character,

Some affluence, if only half-perceived,
In the poverty of their words,
Of the planet of which they were part.

THE RIVER OF RIVERS IN CONNECTICUT

There is a great river this side of Stygia,
Before one comes to the first black cataracts
And trees that lack the intelligence of trees.

In that river, far this side of Stygia,
The mere flowing of the water is a gayety,
Flashing and flashing in the sun. On its banks,

No shadow walks. The river is fateful,
Like the last one. But there is no ferryman.
He could not bend against its propelling force.

It is not to be seen beneath the appearances
That tell of it. The steeple at Farmington
Stands glistening and Haddam shines and sways.

It is the third commonness with light and air,
A curriculum, a vigor, a local abstraction . . .
Call it, once more, a river, an unnamed flowing,

Space-filled, reflecting the seasons, the folk-lore
Of each of the senses; call it, again and again,
The river that flows nowhere, like a sea.

NOT IDEAS ABOUT THE THING BUT THE THING ITSELF

At the earliest ending of winter,
In March, a scrawny cry from outside
Seemed like a sound in his mind.

He knew that he heard it,
A bird's cry, at daylight or before,
In the early March wind.

The sun was rising at six,
No longer a battered panache above snow . . .
It would have been outside.

It was not from the vast ventriloquism
Of sleep's faded papier-mâché . . .
The sun was coming from outside.

That scrawny cry—it was
A chorister whose c preceded the choir.
It was part of the colossal sun,

Surrounded by its choral rings,
Still far away. It was like
A new knowledge of reality.

AS YOU LEAVE THE ROOM

You speak. You say: Today's character is not
A skeleton out of its cabinet. Nor am I.

That poem about the pineapple, the one
About the mind as never satisfied,

The one about the credible hero, the one
About summer, are not what skeletons think about.

I wonder, have I lived a skeleton's life,
As a disbeliever in reality,

A countryman of all the bones in the world?
Now, here, the snow I had forgotten becomes

Part of a major reality, part of
An appreciation of a reality

And thus an elevation, as if I left
With something I could touch, touch every way.

And yet nothing has been changed except what is
Unreal, as if nothing had been changed at all.

THE SICK MAN

Bands of black men seem to be drifting in the air,
In the South, bands of thousands of black men,
Playing mouth-organs in the night or, now, guitars.

Here in the North, late, late, there are voices of men,
Voices in chorus, singing without words, remote and deep,
Drifting choirs, long movements and turnings of sounds.

And in a bed in one room, alone, a listener
Waits for the unison of the music of the drifting bands
And the dissolving chorals, waits for it and imagines

The words of winter in which these two will come together,
In the ceiling of the distant room, in which he lies,
The listener, listening to the shadows, seeing them,

Choosing out of himself, out of everything within him,
Speech for the quiet, good hail of himself, good hail, good hail,
The peaceful, blissful words, well-tuned, well-sung, well-spoken.

THE COURSE OF A PARTICULAR

Today the leaves cry, hanging on branches swept by wind,
Yet the nothingness of winter becomes a little less.
It is still full of icy shades and shapen snow.

The leaves cry . . . One holds off and merely hears the cry.
It is a busy cry, concerning someone else.
And though one says that one is part of everything,

There is a conflict, there is a resistance involved;
And being part is an exertion that declines:
One feels the life of that which gives life as it is.

The leaves cry. It is not a cry of divine attention,
Nor the smoke-drift of puffed-out heroes, nor human cry.
It is the cry of leaves that do not transcend themselves,

In the absence of fantasia, without meaning more
Than they are in the final finding of the ear, in the thing
Itself, until, at last, the cry concerns no one at all.

THE DOVE IN SPRING

Brooder, brooder, deep beneath its walls—
A small howling of the dove
Makes something of the little there,

The little and the dark, and that
In which it is and that in which
It is established. There the dove

Makes this small howling, like a thought
That howls in the mind or like a man
Who keeps seeking out his identity

In that which is and is established . . . It howls
Of the great sizes of an outer bush
And the great misery of the doubt of it,

Of stripes of silver that are strips
Like slits across a space, a place
And state of being large and light.

There is this bubbling before the sun,
This howling at one's ear, too far
For daylight and too near for sleep.

FAREWELL WITHOUT A GUITAR

Spring's bright paradise has come to this.
Now the thousand-leaved green falls to the ground.
Farewell, my days.

The thousand-leaved red
Comes to this thunder of light
At its autumnal terminal—

A Spanish storm,
A wide, still Aragonese,
In which the horse walks home without a rider,

Head down. The reflections and repetitions,
The blows and buffets of fresh senses
Of the rider that was,

Are a final construction,
Like glass and sun, of male reality
And of that other and her desire.

A CHILD ASLEEP IN ITS OWN LIFE

Among the old men that you know,
There is one, unnamed, that broods
On all the rest, in heavy thought.

They are nothing, except in the universe
Of that single mind. He regards them
Outwardly and knows them inwardly,

The sole emperor of what they are,
Distant, yet close enough to wake
The chords above your bed to-night.

TWO LETTERS

I

A LETTER FROM

Even if there had been a crescent moon
On every cloud-tip over the heavens,
Drenching the evening with crystals' light,

One would have wanted more—more—more—
Some true interior to which to return,
A home against one's self, a darkness,

An ease in which to live a moment's life,
The moment of life's love and fortune,
Free from everything else, free above all from thought.

It would have been like lighting a candle,
Like leaning on the table, shading one's eyes,
And hearing a tale one wanted intensely to hear,

As if we were all seated together again
And one of us spoke and all of us believed
What we heard and the light, though little, was enough.

II

A LETTER TO

She wanted a holiday
With someone to speak her dulcied native tongue,

In the shadows of a wood . . .
Shadows, woods . . . and the two of them in speech,

In a secrecy of words
Opened out within a secrecy of place,

Not having to do with love.
A land would hold her in its arms that day

Or something much like a land.
The circle would no longer be broken but closed.

The miles of distance away
From everything would end. It would all meet.

REALITY IS AN ACTIVITY OF THE MOST AUGUST IMAGINATION

Last Friday, in the big light of last Friday night,
We drove home from Cornwall to Hartford, late.

It was not a night blown at a glassworks in Vienna
Or Venice, motionless, gathering time and dust.

There was a crush of strength in a grinding going round,
Under the front of the westward evening star,

The vigor of glory, a glittering in the veins,
As things emerged and moved and were dissolved,

Either in distance, change or nothingness,
The visible transformations of summer night,

An argentine abstraction approaching form
And suddenly denying itself away.

There was an insolid billowing of the solid.
Night's moonlight lake was neither water nor air.

LOCAL OBJECTS

He knew that he was a spirit without a foyer
And that, in this knowledge, local objects become
More precious than the most precious objects of home:

The local objects of a world without a foyer,
Without a remembered past, a present past,
Or a present future, hoped for in present hope,

Objects not present as a matter of course
On the dark side of the heavens or the bright,
In that sphere with so few objects of its own.

Little existed for him but the few things
For which a fresh name always occurred, as if
He wanted to make them, keep them from perishing,

The few things, the objects of insight, the integrations
Of feeling, the things that came of their own accord,
Because he desired without quite knowing what,

That were the moments of the classic, the beautiful.
These were that serene he had always been approaching
As toward an absolute foyer beyond romance.

ARTIFICIAL POPULATIONS

The center that he sought was a state of mind,
Nothing more, like weather after it has cleared—
Well, more than that, like weather when it has cleared
And the two poles continue to maintain it

And the Orient and the Occident embrace
To form that weather's appropriate people,
The rosy men and the women of the rose,
Astute in being what they are made to be.

This artificial population is like
A healing-point in the sickness of the mind:
Like angels resting on a rustic steeple
Or a confect of leafy faces in a tree—

A health—and the faces in a summer night.
So, too, of the races of appropriate people
Of the wind, of the wind as it deepens, and late sleep,
And music that lasts long and lives the more.

A CLEAR DAY AND NO MEMORIES

No soldiers in the scenery,
No thoughts of people now dead,
As they were fifty years ago:
Young and living in a live air,
Young and walking in the sunshine,
Bending in blue dresses to touch something—
Today the mind is not part of the weather.

Today the air is clear of everything.
It has no knowledge except of nothingness
And it flows over us without meanings,
As if none of us had ever been here before
And are not now: in this shallow spectacle,
This invisible activity, this sense.

JULY MOUNTAIN

We live in a constellation
Of patches and of pitches,
Not in a single world,
In things said well in music,
On the piano, and in speech,
As in a page of poetry—
Thinkers without final thoughts
In an always incipient cosmos,
The way, when we climb a mountain,
Vermont throws itself together.

OF MERE BEING

The palm at the end of the mind,
Beyond the last thought, rises
In the bronze decor,

A gold-feathered bird
Sings in the palm, without human meaning,
Without human feeling, a foreign song.

You know then that it is not the reason
That makes us happy or unhappy.
The bird sings. Its feathers shine.

The palm stands on the edge of space.
The wind moves slowly in the branches.
The bird's fire-fangled feathers dangle down.

Short Chronology

1879 Wallace Stevens was born October 2 in Reading, Pennsylvania, the second son of Margaretha, a former teacher, and Garrett Stevens, a lawyer and businessman. Other family members included Garrett Jr., born December 19, 1877; John, born December 9, 1880; Elizabeth, born July 19, 1885; and Mary Katharine, born April 25, 1889.

1885–91 Although raised Presbyterian, Stevens attended Lutheran grammar schools and studied, among other subjects, French and German, which he continued to read throughout his life.

1892–1897 Stevens took the classical curriculum at Reading Boys' High School and, after being held back one year due to illness and low grades, he graduated with merit, having won prizes for writing and public speaking.

1897–1900 Stevens attended Harvard College as a special student in a three-year nondegree program, taking most of his coursework in English, French, and German languages and literature. He published more than thirty poems, short stories, and sketches in the *Harvard Advocate* and *Harvard Monthly*, often under pseudonyms, and served as secretary of the Signet Society and president of the *Harvard Advocate*.

1900–1901 After leaving Harvard, Stevens tried his hand at journalism, writing for the *New York Tribune* and *World's Work*, a monthly magazine, but he found the work unfulfilling.

1901–1903 Influenced by his father, a lawyer, Stevens enrolled at New York Law School. During the summer of 1902, he clerked for W. G. Peckham, a New York attorney. He graduated from law school in June 1903. Employed by Peckham as a law clerk, Stevens accompanied him on an unforgettable seven-week hunting trip to British Columbia in late summer 1903.

1904 Admitted to the New York bar in June 1904, Stevens visited his home in Pennsylvania, where he met Elsie Kachel, who had been born in Reading on June 5, 1886. Thus began a five-year courtship, carried on mostly in correspondence, while Stevens struggled financially as a lawyer in New York, moving from firm to firm.

1908   In January, Stevens secured a position with the American Bonding Company, which initiated his lifelong legal specialty in the insurance business. In June, he sent Elsie "A Book of Verses," composed for her twenty-second birthday. Despite his family's objections to her lower social status, they became engaged at Christmas. This created an irreparable rift with his family.

1909   For her twenty-third birthday, Stevens composed another collection of poems for Elsie, "The Little June Book." They were married on September 21 in Reading, with none of Stevens's family in attendance. They moved to New York and remained there until their move to Hartford, Connecticut, in 1916.

1911   Stevens's father died in Reading on July 14, and Stevens attended the funeral. He had not spoken with his father since their argument over Elsie in 1908.

1912   Stevens's mother died in Reading on July 16, and Stevens attended the funeral.

1914   Stevens joined the New York office of the Equitable Surety Company in February as a vice president. He began to publish minor poems, including two poetic sequences, "Carnet de Voyage" and "Phases." His return to poetry was in part stimulated by his financial stability and by the group of writers, artists, and musicians, such as William Carlos Williams and Marcel Duchamp, who gathered regularly at Walter Arensberg's New York apartment.

1915   Stevens published his first mature poems, "Peter Quince at the Clavier" and "Sunday Morning."

1916   Invited to join the Hartford Accident and Indemnity Company, where soon thereafter he became head of the surety bond department, Stevens and Elsie moved permanently to Hartford. Specializing in fidelity and surety claims, he traveled extensively throughout the United States, visiting places such as Florida, Oklahoma, and Minnesota—landscapes that began to appear in his early poetry. Trying his hand at drama, he won the $100 *Poetry* prize for *Three Travelers Watch a Sunrise*. Elsie's profile served as the image of Mercury on the American dime through the mid-1940s.

1917   Although he did not attend its solo production, his verse play *Carlos Among the Candles* was performed in an Off-Broadway theater in New York. He composed a third verse drama around this time: *Bowl, Cat and Broomstick*.

1919   In May, Mary Katharine, Stevens's youngest sister, died in France while serving as a Red Cross volunteer during and after World War I.

1920   *Three Travelers Watch a Sunrise* was performed once by the Provincetown Players in New York in February, but Stevens did not attend. He won the Levinson Prize from *Poetry* for a group of poems, "Pecksniffiana," in November.

1921   Stevens submitted "From the Journal of Crispin" for the Blindman Prize, sponsored by the Poetry Society of South Carolina, and received first honorable mention from the sole judge, Amy Lowell. He revised the poem as "The Comedian as the Letter C."

1923   In September, shortly before his forty-fourth birthday, Stevens published his first book, *Harmonium,* with Alfred A. Knopf. He and Elsie took their first extended vacation, traveling to Havana, the Panama Canal, the Gulf of Tehuantepec, California, and overland back to Hartford.

1924   Holly Bright Stevens, his only child, was born on August 10 in Hartford.

1925–1933   Claiming the new baby and work consumed his energies, Stevens virtually stopped writing poetry.

1931   Knopf reissued *Harmonium* in a revised edition (three poems were deleted, and fourteen, most composed before 1924, were added). Stevens started a lifelong relationship with a Parisian bookseller, Anatole Vidal, and later with his daughter, Paule Vidal, from whom he purchased books and paintings.

1932   In September, Stevens moved to 118 Westerly Terrace in Hartford, the only home he ever owned, located near Elizabeth Park.

1934   Stevens was named vice president of Hartford Accident and Indemnity Company in February at a salary (during this year of the Depression) of $17,500. (Based on the Consumer Price Index for 2008, its modern equivalent would be $281,500.)

1935   *Ideas of Order* was published in a limited edition by Alcestis Press in August.

1936   In February in Key West, a somewhat intoxicated Stevens insulted Ernest Hemingway and a fistfight ensued; Stevens broke his hand on Hemingway's jaw, but the two made amends and concealed the cause of the injury (Stevens claimed he fell down some stairs). In October, Knopf published a trade edition of *Ideas of Order.* In November, Stevens won *The Nation*'s Poetry Prize for "The Men That Are Falling." Also in November, the Alcestis Press issued a limited edition of *Owl's Clover.* In December, Stevens delivered a lecture, "The Irrational Element in Poetry," at Harvard, his first essay on the theory of poetry.

1937   In October, Knopf published *The Man with the Blue Guitar & Other Poems.* Stevens's older brother, Garrett Jr., a lawyer in Cleveland, died in November. Stevens provided financial support to his brother's family during his illness and after his death.

1940   Stevens's younger brother, John, also a lawyer, died in July in Philadelphia.

1941   Stevens read "The Noble Rider and the Sound of Words" at Princeton University in May. He initiated genealogical studies that engaged him for the rest of his life.

1942   In September, Knopf published *Parts of a World.* In October, the Cummington Press published a limited edition of *Notes toward a Supreme Fiction.*

1943   In February, Stevens's last surviving sibling, Elizabeth Stevens MacFarland, died in Philadelphia. In August, he read "The Figure of the Youth as Virile Poet" at Mount Holyoke College.

1944   Against Stevens's objections, Holly married John Hanchak, a repairman, in August.

1945   In June, Stevens read "Description Without Place" as the Phi Beta Kappa poem at Harvard. In November, the Cummington Press published *Esthétique du Mal* in a limited edition. Stevens was elected to the National Institute of Arts and Letters in December and inducted in May 1946.

1947   In February, Stevens read his essay "Three Academic Pieces" at Harvard. *Transport to Summer* was published by Knopf in March. His only grandchild, Peter Reed Hanchak, was born on April 26. Stevens received an honorary doctorate from Wesleyan University in June. Also in June, the Cummington Press published *Three Academic Pieces* in a limited edition.

1948   At Yale University in March and Mount Holyoke in April, Stevens read his essay "Effects of Analogy." In September, he read "Imagination as Value" at Columbia University.

1949   In September, Stevens received *Still Life* by Pierre Tal-Coat from his Parisian art dealer, which inspired him to write "Angel Surrounded by Paysans." In November, he read "An Ordinary Evening in New Haven" at the 150th celebration of the Connecticut Academy of Arts and Sciences in New Haven.

1950   In March, Stevens was awarded the Bollingen Prize in Poetry for 1949. In September, Knopf published *The Auroras of Autumn*.

1951   In January, Stevens delivered his lecture "The Relations Between Poetry and Painting" at the Museum of Modem Art in New York. Later that month, also in New York, he was awarded the Gold Medal of the Poetry Society of America. In March, he garnered the 1950 National Book Award in Poetry for *The Auroras of Autumn*. He received an honorary doctorate from Bard College in March and read his essay "Two or Three Ideas" at Mount Holyoke in April. In June, he received an honorary degree from Harvard. Holly Stevens was granted a divorce from John Hanchak in September. In November, Knopf published *The Necessary Angel: Essays on Reality and the Imagination*. Stevens presented a lecture, "A Collect of Philosophy," at the University of Chicago and at City College of New York.

1952   In June, Stevens received honorary doctorates from Mount Holyoke and Columbia.

1953   In February, Faber and Faber published *Selected Poems* in England, his first official recognition in that country.

1954   Stevens made a recording of some of his poems for Harvard Library. In May, he presented "The Sail of Ulysses" as the Phi Beta Kappa poem at Columbia. In October, on the occasion of his seventy-fifth birthday, Knopf released *The Collected Poems of Wallace Stevens*.

1955   In January, Stevens received the National Book Award in Poetry for 1954 for *The Collected Poems*. In April, he was diagnosed with inoperable cancer of the stomach. Awarded the Pulitzer Prize in Poetry in May, he received two more honorary doctorates, one from Hartt College of Music, in Hartford, and the other from Yale in June. Stevens died on August 2 at St. Francis Hospital in Hartford and was buried at Cedar Hill Cemetery in Hartford.

1963   Elsie Stevens died on February 19 in Hartford.

1992   Holly Stevens died on March 4 in Guilford, Connecticut.

Suggestions for Further Reading

Biographical Studies

Bates, Milton J. *Wallace Stevens: A Mythology of Self.* Berkeley: University of California Press, 1985.

Brazeau, Peter. *Parts of a World: Wallace Stevens Remembered—An Oral Biography.* New York: Random House, 1983.

Crockett, John. "Of Holly and Wallace Stevens in a Purple Light." *Wallace Stevens Journal* 21.1 (1997): 3–33.

Gaddis, Eugene R. "Poets of Life and the Imagination: Wallace Stevens and Chick Austin." *Wallace Stevens Journal* 28.2 (2004): 261–78.

Lensing, George S. *Wallace Stevens: A Poet's Growth.* Baton Rouge: Louisiana State University Press, 1986.

Richardson, Joan. *Wallace Stevens: The Early Years, 1879–1923.* New York: William Morrow, 1986.

———. *Wallace Stevens: The Later Years, 1923–1955.* New York: William Morrow, 1988.

Sharpe, Tony. *Wallace Stevens: A Literary Life.* New York: St. Martin's Press, 1999.

Stevens, Holly. "Bits of Remembered Time." *Southern Review* 7 n.s. 3 (1971): 651–7.

———. *Souvenirs and Prophecies: The Young Wallace Stevens.* New York: Knopf, 1977.

Selected Criticism

Bloom, Harold. *Wallace Stevens: The Poems of Our Climate.* Ithaca: Cornell University Press, 1977.

Brogan, Jacqueline Vaught. *Stevens and Simile: A Theory of Language.* Princeton: Princeton University Press, 1986.

Carroll, Joseph. *Wallace Stevens' Supreme Fiction: A New Romanticism.* Baton Rouge: Louisiana State University Press, 1987.

Cook, Eleanor. *Poetry, Word-Play, and Word-War in Wallace Stevens.* Princeton: Princeton University Press, 1988.

Critchley, Simon. *Things Merely Are: Philosophy in the Poetry of Wallace Stevens.* London: Routledge, 2005.

Doggett, Frank. *Stevens' Poetry of Thought.* Baltimore: Johns Hopkins Press, 1966.

Doggett, Frank, and Robert Buttel, eds. *Wallace Stevens: A Celebration.* Princeton: Princeton University Press, 1980.

Filreis, Alan. *Wallace Stevens and the Actual World.* Princeton: Princeton University Press, 1991.

Gelpi, Albert, ed. *Wallace Stevens: The Poetics of Modernism.* Cambridge: Cambridge University Press, 1985.

Grey, Thomas C. *The Wallace Stevens Case: Law and the Practice of Poetry.* Cambridge: Harvard University Press, 1991.

Leggett, B. J. *Late Stevens: The Final Fiction.* Baton Rouge: Louisiana State University Press, 2005.

Lensing, George S. *Wallace Stevens and the Seasons.* Baton Rouge: Louisiana State University Press, 2001.

Litz, A. Walton. *Introspective Voyager: The Poetic Development of Wallace Stevens.* New York: Oxford University Press, 1972.

Longenbach, James. *Wallace Stevens: The Plain Sense of Things.* New York: Oxford University Press, 1991.

MacLeod, Glen G. *Wallace Stevens and Modern Art: From the Armory Show to Abstract Expressionism.* New Haven: Yale University Press, 1993.

McCann, Janet. *Wallace Stevens Revisited: "The Celestial Possible."* New York: Twayne, 1995.

Maeder, Beverly. *Wallace Stevens' Experimental Language: The Lion in the Lute.* New York: St. Martin's Press, 1999.

Rehder, Robert. *The Poetry of Wallace Stevens.* New York: St. Martin's Press, 1988.

Riddel, Joseph N. *The Clairvoyant Eye: The Poetry and Poetics of Wallace Stevens.* Baton Rouge: Louisiana State University Press, 1965; rpt. 1991.

Serio, John N., ed. *The Cambridge Companion to Wallace Stevens.* Cambridge: Cambridge University Press, 2007.

Serio, John N., and B. J. Leggett. *Teaching Wallace Stevens: Practical Essays.* Knoxville: University of Tennessee Press, 1994.

Vendler, Helen. *Wallace Stevens: Words Chosen Out of Desire.* Knoxville: University of Tennessee Press, 1984; rpt. Cambridge: Harvard University Press, 1986.

Reference Materials

Cook, Eleanor. *A Reader's Guide to Wallace Stevens.* Princeton: Princeton University Press, 2007.

Edelstein, J. M. *Wallace Stevens: A Descriptive Bibliography.* Pittsburgh: University of Pittsburgh Press, 1973.

Serio, John N. *Wallace Stevens: An Annotated Secondary Bibliography.* Pittsburgh: University of Pittsburgh Press, 1994.

Serio, John N., and Greg Foster. *Online Concordance to Wallace Stevens' Poetry.* 2009. http://www.wallacestevens.com.

Sukenick, Ronald. *Wallace Stevens: Musing the Obscure—Readings, An Interpretation and a Guide to the Collected Poetry.* New York: New York University Press, 1967.

Index of Titles

A NOTE ON THE TYPE

This book was set in a version of Monotype Baskerville, the antecedent of which was a typeface designed by John Baskerville (1706–1775). Baskerville, a writing master in Birmingham, England, began experimenting around 1750 with type design and punch cutting. His first book, published in 1757 and set throughout in his new types, was a Virgil in royal quarto. It was followed by other famous editions from his press. Baskerville's types, which are distinctive and elegant in design, were a forerunner of what we know today as the "modern" group of typefaces.

Composed by Creative Graphics,
Allentown, Pennsylvania

Printed and bound by R. R. Donnelley,
Crawfordsville, Indiana